THE SOCIAL STUDIES IN ENGLISH EDUCATION

THE SOCIAL STUDIES IN ENGLISH EDUCATION

Vincent R. Rogers

Professor of Education
University of Connecticut

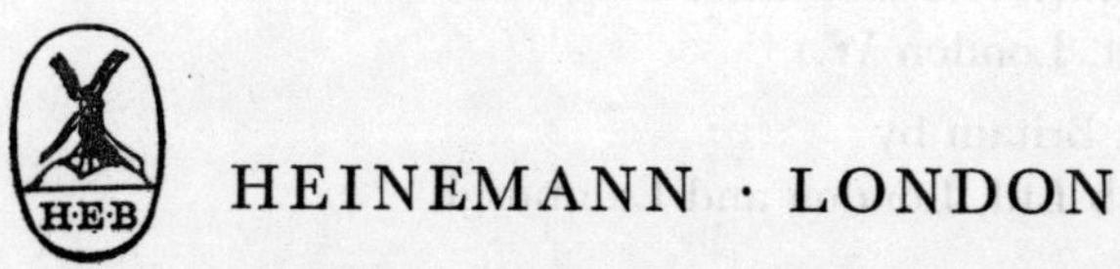

HEINEMANN · LONDON

Heinemann Educational Books Ltd

LONDON MELBOURNE TORONTO
SINGAPORE AUCKLAND JOHANNESBURG
HONG KONG NAIROBI IBADAN

SBN 435 80760 9
© Vincent R. Rogers 1968
First published 1968

Published by Heinemann Educational Books Ltd
48 Charles Street, London W.1
Printed in Great Britain by
Morrison & Gibb Ltd, London and Edinburgh

CONTENTS

PREFACE

John Haymes Holmes once warned that, 'the life of humanity upon this planet may yet come to ... a very terrible end. But I would have you notice that this end is threatened in our time not by anything that the universe may do to us, but only by what man may do to himself'. As one looks into the future it seems that, more and more, man's fate is likely to depend not so much upon his technology—his skills—the degree to which he is 'literate' or 'numerate'—but rather upon the way he chooses to use or apply such skills.

The wise and just application of technological knowledge about the physical universe, then depends upon man's understanding of himself as an individual and of the many groups to which he belongs and relates. If one accepts this notion, it becomes increasingly clear that the *social* education of the world's children and youth is of crucial importance to twentieth century man in *all* societies, Western and non-Western, developed and developing. It is in this spirit that this study was undertaken.

The literature of Education contains surprisingly little in the way of descriptive or comparative studies of the nature of social education in a variety of countries. We know a great deal about problems related to literacy, but very little about the ways in which the nations of the world attempt to produce 'citizens' (however defined) who will lead productive, meaningful lives in a given society. It is exceedingly difficult for the comparative educator to obtain specific examples of curricula, syllabuses, and other classroom materials related to a given nation's efforts in the field of social education, and reasonably comprehensive studies involving first-hand observation of classroom practice are even more difficult to find.

This study, then, is an attempt both to describe and evaluate the social education of English primary and secondary school children. I visited more than 70 schools—selective and non-selective, state supported and privately maintained—talked to hundreds of students, teachers, administrators and others, and examined dozens of curriculum guides, syllabuses, textbooks, examinations, and other teaching material. Hopefully, I have succeeded in synthesizing this kind of 'data' into a reasonably accurate image of the goals and practices as well as the strengths and weaknesses of this aspect of English Education. The work has been generously supported by the Office of International Programs at the University of Minnesota, Kappa Delta Pi, and the Fulbright Program of the State Department of the United States.

I have also benefited from the advice and assistance of friends and associates (both here and abroad) too numerous to name. Particular thanks go, however, to my English colleagues R. Irvine Smith at York University, and Dennis Lawton at the University of London who read and criticized the manuscript, and Maurice Kogan of the Department of Education and Science who helped pave the way for the school visitation upon which this study depended.

University of Connecticut   VINCENT R. ROGERS

INTRODUCTION

WHEN A British Member of Parliament speaks in the House of Commons about a proposal to which he may be personally committed, he often prefaces his remarks by 'declaring his interest'; that is, he warns his colleagues that in this instance he cannot be entirely objective or free from some form of personal bias. I would like to begin by 'declaring my interest' in social studies; or, more precisely, in the social sciences from which 'social studies' derive.

The effectiveness of formal education, i.e., one's experiences in the classrooms of those institutions we label 'schools', is, of course, uncertain. One becomes what one becomes because of the influence of institutions as obvious as the family and the church, and as subtle as the nuances, gestures and intonations of dozens of individuals with whom we come in contact—both directly and (increasingly) vicariously.

Nevertheless, the school exists, and during the years between five and sixteen it plays a significant role in the socialization and education of any normal child. Our perceptions of the physical world in which we live; our attitudes toward the growing and diverse masses of people who inhabit it; the goals we strive toward and the 'crimes' we condemn—all are to some extent effected by the schooling we receive.

If we can accept the notion that formal education is not a negligible influence in one's journey from childhood to maturity, it seems reasonable (given the nature of the twentieth-century world in which we find ourselves) that growing numbers of educators and laymen should become concerned about those aspects of the school curriculum that are directly concerned with the study of man and society—that is, the social studies.

For our purposes, let us conceive of 'social studies' as being concerned fundamentally with *man* both as an individual and as a member of a host of groups; with *man* both changing and adjusting to his environment. The content, the 'meat' of such studies will be drawn largely from the disciplines of geography, history, sociology, anthropology, political science, economics, and, to some extent, psychology and philosophy. However, the term 'social studies' will be used here as a broad organizing concept rather than as a description of a given 'course'. That is, one school's social studies program may consist of a series of courses that are quite clearly history and geography. Another school may have developed a broad, integrated program for a particular form or year, while still requiring the study of history and geography as separate subjects at other times. A school might offer a humanities course, or perhaps, a general studies course that would include aspects of the study of man and society, as well as more formal courses in sociology and economics. In other words, we are concerned here with the study of man and society, regardless of specific course titles or other (often diverting) labels.

Another word of caution and clarification: many English schools engage in a host of activities that might broadly be classified as 'social education'. I refer, of course, to those programs involving visits to the elderly and disabled, job and career information programs, holiday cruises to foreign lands, etc. For our purposes, these activities (as important as they often are) will be considered as peripheral to our main concern. This analysis deals essentially with how the school attempts to expose children to certain facts, ideas, concepts and generalizations about man interacting with his fellow-man and with the environment—that is, we are concerned with the school's *systematic* and formal attempts to help children understand the social world in which they live.

Those readers who have kept abreast of educational developments in England during the last five or six years will be well aware that this is an unusually active, occasionally exciting, and often confusing period. English education finds itself going through an 'agonizing reappraisal', and heated, often bitter debate is going on simultaneously over a number of issues, ranging all the way from primary school class size to the relationship between universities and colleges of education. A host of reports—Newsom, Robbins, Crowther, Plowden—have emerged almost at once, each calling for its own brand of reform, and each raising a score of excruciatingly significant questions that will affect education here for generations to come. In a society that places an unusual value on tradition, continuity and gradualism, the call for so much reform in so short a period of time seems almost diabolically upsetting.

Similarly, Americans find themselves debating the merits of flexible scheduling, team-teaching, and non-graded schools. The education of urban and rural deprived children is undergoing a minor revolution and there is anything but universal agreement concerning the best ways of improving their education. Other unresolved and widely discussed issues in the United States have to do with the nature of the evolving relationship between the federal government and local education authorities, the increasingly militant tactics used by organized groups of teachers as they seek higher wages and better working conditions, and the controversial question of state aid to private schools—a question which is complicated by the fact that such aid in America usually means state aid to schools with some sort of religious affiliation or commitment.

It would of course, be foolish to argue that separation of church and state (in America) is a more important problem than is the question of how best to educate our deprived youth. Neither can we say with any certainty that limiting the size of primary school classes in England is more important than improving the education of teachers. Nevertheless, I would like to suggest that the crucial educational question of our times on either side of the Atlantic is and will continue to be for at least the next decade *the nature and direction taken by what might be called 'The Curriculum Revolution'*.

The Madison (U.S.A.) Mathematics Project, the Nuffield Junior Science Project, the Math and Science Programs developed by the Educational Development Center at Cambridge, Mass., the new Humanities Programme just begun by Nuffield and the Schools Council—all of these projects address themselves to what Americans would call the 'blood and guts' problems of Education, i.e., what should be taught to children and how should we do it?

Surely these are the issues that concern me most, and these are the issues with which this study will attempt to deal. Essentially, I will discuss the following questions:

1. What is taught about man and society in English primary and secondary schools?

2. How is this done?

3. Do existing curricula and teaching methods in the social studies appear to be adequate for today's world and appropriate for today's children? If so, how? If not, why not?

4. If existing programs are not beyond criticism, how might they be improved?

5. What are some new trends and developments both in England and in the United States that may be likely to effect the shape and substance of new social studies curricula?

Ralph Tyler, who recently retired as Director of the Center for Advanced Study in Behavorial Sciences at Stanford, California, likes to tell the story of the empiricist, who, doubting the effectiveness of Christian baptism, decided upon the birth of his twin sons to baptize one and keep the other as a control. The reader may rest assured that this sort of scientific objectivity has not been utilized in this study. It is, unfortunately and at best, a highly subjective work based upon my personal analysis of data obtained in interviews, school visits, and the reading of syllabuses, textbooks and other related materials. Given these limitations, I have nevertheless rushed in where angels fear to tread—keeping always in the back of my mind, however, a personalized paraphrase of Cromwell's admonition to 'Think in the Bowels of Christ—*You May Be Mistaken!*'

I: THE DEVELOPMENT OF SOCIAL STUDIES IN ENGLISH EDUCATION

SINCE WE have defined 'social studies' in broad, inclusive terms, it seems reasonable that this section should include at least a brief treatment of the development of what has been, traditionally, the 'mainstream' of English social education, i.e., history and geography. Some attention will also be paid to the development of sociology and economics as school subjects. Considerably more space, however, will be devoted to the emergence, decline, and partial renaissance of integrated courses that are labeled, quite specifically, 'social studies'.

History

While history, too, had to battle for a place in the academic sun against such formidable opponents as Greek and Latin, it entered the lists far earlier than did the other social studies with which we are concerned. And, since Englishmen are probably no less curious about their origins than other people (and possibly are considerably more so than most), it is quite likely that some form of history teaching has existed here so long as there was someone to talk and someone to listen. We know that the first English history 'textbook' (called *The History of England from 1450–1509*) appeared during the reign of Queen Elizabeth and that something called *Historical Questions*, written by a London teacher named Richmal Mangall was published as early as 1804.[1]

It was not, however, until later in the nineteenth century that history emerged as an identifiable school subject, and not

[1] *The Teaching of History in Secondary Schools*, issued by The Incorporated Association of Assistant Masters in Secondary Schools. Cambridge: Cambridge University Press, 1965, p. 1.

until 1838 that the first public examination in history was offered by the University of London. Probably it was the establishment of history at Oxford and Cambridge in 1872 and 1874, respectively, that brought an unquestioned, 'official' blessing to it as a school subject, and by the late nineteenth century it was regularly taught and firmly established in a number of grammar schools.[1] Indeed, in the examinations of the London, Oxford, and Cambridge Examining Boards of 1890, 91 per cent of the 75,000 candidates took the history examination.[2]

By 1900 it would be fair to say that history had become a widely accepted, respected, 'traditional', and entrenched offering in the curriculum of most English secondary schools and universities.

History's place was somewhat less firmly established in primary schools, however, due to the changing conceptions of the discipline that were emerging at the time. The 'new' historians (such as Lord Acton and J. B. Bury of Cambridge) were confident that history was well on its way to becoming a 'science'. This meant, of course, that the simplistic, almost catechismic approach to history that had made it appear suitable (in varying quantities) to children at almost any age could no longer justifiably be followed. Complexities like Cause and Effect began to clutter up the history books, and there was considerable doubt about pre-secondary school children's ability to deal profitably with this new brand of history.

Nevertheless, at this point in time, history (however scattered, incidental or informal) is taught in most English junior schools. It is offered at all levels and in all types of secondary schools, and of course, its place in college and university courses of study goes largely unchallenged.

Geography

The development of geography follows a somewhat similar path. While it did not emerge as a school subject until later in

---

[1] *Teaching History*, Pamphlet No. 23, London: Her Majesty's Stationery Office, 1952, p. 8.

[2] *The Teaching of History in Secondary Schools*, p. 2.

the nineteenth century (instruction was more or less incidental prior to this time), there is evidence that it was taught at the Mathematical School of Christ's Hospital as early as 1673, 'mainly for its usefulness in the training of seamen'.[1] By 1891 geography lecturers or readers were appointed at Oxford, Cambridge, and Manchester Universities, and it became apparent that geography, too, had achieved its aura of respectability —although its position is not quite as solid as is that of history. One does hear criticism, for example, related to geography's 'lack of rigor', scientific 'pretensions', and inappropriateness for 'really able' students. Nevertheless, geography has earned a far more respectable place for itself in England than in America at virtually all levels of education. It appears (often in the form of carefully and effectively devised programs of local or environmental studies) in practically all junior schools, and it is generally required at least for the first two years of secondary school. It is clearly one of the more popular G.C.E. choices at both ordinary and advanced level, and it is a 'main course' option at almost all colleges of education. With faculties at Oxford, Cambridge, and London Universities, its place at this level of education seems assured.

The Development of 'Social Studies' as a School Subject

The possibility that the social sciences might have a significant role to play in helping modern man shape and improve the society in which he lives is not a new idea in England. Indeed, as early as 1850 an organization called 'The National Association for the Promotion of Social Science' was organized. Neither were concepts about 'integrated' courses of study or courses emphasizing the inter-relatedness of knowledge about man and society unknown during the post World War I period. (One might look at the Institute of Sociology and the International Students Service's 'Joint Report' for 1936, for example, which is entitled *The Social Sciences: Their Relations in Theory and Practice*.)

Integrated 'social studies' courses for the schools, however,

[1] *Geography and Education*, Ministry of Education, Pamphlet No. 39, London: Her Majesty's Stationery Office, 1960, p. 10.

received their major impetus with the passing of the Education Act of 1944. This landmark in the history of English education eventually raised the school leaving age to fifteen years and therefore called for secondary education for *all*, rather than for the intellectually able alone. Most education authorities adopted a tripartite, selective system of education, and the Secondary Modern School was born.

The sudden introduction into secondary education of large numbers of children representing *all* ability ranges presented obvious and traumatic problems. Pleas were made for 'practicality' and 'relevance' in the education of 'non-academic' children, and for some form of 'social studies' as a substitute for traditional, bookish, often dull and lack-lustre history and geography.

At the same time, the influence of educational progressives such as Dewey, Montessori and Rousseau began to have its effect, and comments like these appeared increasingly in education journals:

> The aim of the modern school is to provide a good all-round secondary education, not focused primarily on the traditional subjects of the school curriculum, but developing out of the interests of the children.
>
> . . . the schools must concentrate attention on securing a balanced and harmonious development in which there is not undue emphasis on intellectual growth, but in which intellectual growth is seen merely as one facet of the whole child. The child's social, emotional, physical and spiritual development demands equally serious consideration. . . . No claim is made that they are the unique concern of the Modern school. But the Modern school of the future must go considerably further in giving scope to these sides of a child's development than schools have commonly done in the past.[1]

Children were now to learn from 'experience' and would, of course, be freed from the shackles of examinations.

Another impetus for change in the study of man and society came from pressure groups such as the Association for Education in Citizenship, as well as from widely shared, general reactions to war itself, which encouraged the notion that the

[1] W. Taylor, *The Secondary Modern School*. London: Faber and Faber, 1963, p. 96.

schools ought somehow to do their bit toward creating a much more civilized post-war world.[1]

In essence, then, the social studies had achieved in the early fifties a tenuous, tentative acceptance as a school subject appropriate, at least, for less academically able children. Its nature, form, or structure was perhaps exemplified by statements like the following:

> What we now call Social Studies . . . is a synthesis: a broad highway to a working knowledge of Life in its widest sense. The quality of Social Studies differs from the isolated subject teaching . . . in being Discovery . . . of those aspects of life related to the experience of children.[2]

Perhaps these excerpts from a social studies syllabus for secondary schools which was intended to replace history, geography, and civics illustrate the point in more practical terms:

SOCIAL STUDIES

Boys and Girls

A rapid outline of how children live and what they do. This will give a broad outline of both History and Geography against which details may later be seen in perspective.

Boys and girls in England: now—in 1938 (father's time)—in 1914 (grandfather's time)—in 1840 (grandfather's grandfather's time) —in 1666—in 1485—in feudal days—Saxon times—Roman England—Pre-Roman. (Only fourteen generations back to Henry VIII.) Boys and girls in other lands: Canada—China—Australia—India—Italy—Norway.

Clothes

Now—in 1938—1921—1914—1840—1750—1666—1485—1097 —and before. Where clothes are made, and why in those places. Raw materials and where they come from. Influence of geography on clothes.

---

[1] C. Cannon, 'Social Studies in Secondary Schools', *Education Review*, Volume 17, No. 1, November 1964, p. 20. (This is an excellent article which treats the history of the social studies movement in England in considerable detail.)

[2] F. J. Nicholson, *Some Suggestions For Teachers of Social Studies in Post-Primary Classes*. 1949, p. 5, quoted in Canon, p. 21.

Houses

Prefabs — pre war — Victorian — Georgian — Jacobean — Elizabethan — Tudor — Norman — Roman.

Districts of England and types of houses—raw materials available and climatic considerations.

Towns and Villages

Our own town or village. Nearby towns and villages. Why towns are where they are. History of our own part of the country, and how its people live. Chief towns of British Isles—why they are there and what they do. Place-names and their origin. (This work will include such map-making and map-reading together with history, which will bear largely on Roman, Saxon, and Danish times and on the Industrial Revolution.) New towns— town and country planning.

Earning a Living

Main industries of Great Britain and their location. Relation between industry, location of raw materials, climate, communications. Raw materials from overseas and their transport.

Effects of Industrial Revolution, illustrated by reference to nearest industrial town only. How people earn their living: today—1900—1850—1820—1750.

Ways of earning a living: primary industries—secondary industries—services. Goods for home use, goods for export.

Going to the Post Office

An example of a state service. What the Post Office does—history of post in England.

Sending a letter abroad—how it travels—world communications and Empire communications in particular.

Local Government

Electing a committee to run the local authority 'club'.

History of local government, showing steady increase of matters which the local authority now handles on behalf of the individual.

List exactly the services provided by the local authority and whom to approach on any matters involving locally provided services.[1]

By 1955, however, the social studies star was already in decline, if indeed it had ever really ascended. The National Association of Schoolmasters, upon polling its members concerning the general progress of the Secondary Modern School, found comments like these appearing all too frequently—comments which hinted at the development of an education climate which was anything but healthy for the social studies:

> Education Stunts and Theories over the past few years have tended to keep standards down.
> More will to work is needed. Too much time is being spent in experimenting and too little in teaching and learning a solid core of subjects.[2]

By the late 1950's this brave new enthusiasm had all but died, and history and geography were again in command.

Hostility to the Development of Social Studies as a School Subject

In contrast to American experience, hostility to the social studies idea in England was far more prevalent, considerably more pointed, infinitely better expressed, and (consequently) exceedingly effective. An analysis of the origins and nature of this negative reaction follows.

Some resistance to change occurs in almost all societies. The jump from the known to the unknown is perceived by most normal people as hazardous, and the tendency to muddle through with something like the *status quo* is not restricted to the English. Nevertheless, inertia seems to play a more influential role in hindering English educational reform than it does, say, in the United States, the Soviet Union, or in Scandinavia. Resistance to the social studies, then, might be expected just as there was resistance to the 'natural sciences' when they emerged upon the educational scene. Any new area of study, any new discipline faces an arduous, tortuous journey to academic

[1] J. Mander, *Old Bottles and New Wine*. London: Newnes Educational Publishing Company, 1948, pp. 97–101.

[2] Quoted in W. Taylor, *The Secondary Modern School*. London: Faber and Faber, 1963, p. 99.

respectability in England. It is, after all, only recently (the early 1960's) that Sociology has been offered at Oxford and Cambridge.

Similarly, there remains in the scholar's world a residual feeling that the social sciences are not really quite respectable academically. This feeling was briefly and pointedly expressed by a group of sixth form masters who were responding to a questionnaire dealing with the possible inclusion of more social science in the curriculum of the sixth form. In summarizing their objections, they concluded, 'We doubt whether the social sciences are sufficient intellectual disclipine to justify the displacement of more conventional school subjects.'[1]

The limited role that social studies and social science have played (up to quite recently) at English colleges and universities led, naturally enough, to a lack of familiarity with and respect for these disciplines among the teachers educated at these institutions. (At this writing it seems fair to say that social science *still* plays a relatively minor role in the education of teachers, and this lack cannot help but be reflected in teachers' attitudes toward school subjects derived from or related to social science.)

Another factor that accounts for some of the resistance to social studies in England must be the rather stand-offish attitude of university political scientists, anthropologists, sociologists, and others toward what goes on in the lower schools. We find little here of the push given to American developments in the social studies by learned societies such as the American Sociological Association or by individuals such as the University of Chicago's renowned political scientist David Easton, Purdue University economist Lawrence Senesh, or Syracuse University geographer Preston James. The English attitude is often expressed as follows: 'my discipline is too complex to be handled at any lower level of education—don't worry about it until the student comes to the university'—forgetting, of course, that only a handful will eventually arrive, and only a small portion of that handful will actually engage in serious study of a given social science.

University academicians in the social sciences as a group,

---

[1] G. E. Hurd, 'Sociology For Sixth Formers?' *Educational Review*, Volume 11, No. 3, January 1965, pp. 198–212.

then, seem to be surprisingly unaware of and unconcerned about the activities of primary and secondary schools—and those working toward curricular reform in the schools have found minimal interest and support from their university colleagues.

Another, related, problem is the tendency here for subjects to vie with one another for status. (A problem, incidentally, not restricted to English education.) One sees considerable activity on the curriculum development front in terms of separate disciplines, but (apart from the primary schools) there seems to be little effort made to develop curriculum on a broad, school-wide basis. The geography staff revises its syllabus, as do their colleagues in history, English and maths. If a strong enough case can be made for additional time in a crowded time-table for a given subject, this may well be done—often at the expense of a less favored (or perhaps less well defended) subject. In any event, to the historians, history comes first—as does maths for the mathematicians, chemistry for the chemists, and Greek and Latin for the classicists. It is sort of an academic skirmish, and to the victors belong the spoils.

Perhaps still another explanation for social studies' lack of general acceptance in England has to do with the nature of the educational system as a whole—in particular the role played by external examinations. Quite obviously, examined subjects are those which traditionally are held in greatest esteem. Bryan, writing in the recently published *Frontiers in Geographic Thought* complains that 'examination syllabuses dictate more than anything else what we teach in schools'.[1] The overwhelming majority of teachers to whom I spoke seemed essentially to concur with this view. Social studies is *not* now an examined subject for the General Certificate of Education. History and geography (and more recently economics and sociology) *are* so examined—therefore 'social studies' (for this and for other reasons) continues to play a relatively minor role in English education. (The results of a *New Society*[2] survey conducted in

[1] R. C. Charley and P. Haggett, Editors, *Frontiers in Geographic Thought.* London: Methuen and Company, Ltd,. 1965, see chapter XVI by P. Bryan, p. 330.

[2] 'School Social Studies', *New Society*, Volume 4, No. 101, 3rd September 1964, p. 4.

late 1964 indicate that many heads would like to include social studies/social science offerings, yet they feel that external examinations preclude that possibility.)

Closely related to this, of course, is the problem of university admittance requirements. Since two G.C.E. advanced level passes are the current *minimum* requirement (*three* passes at A level seem to be required in *practice*, however), there is little inclination to take non-examinable courses very seriously. Ample time exists in most typical school time-tables, but it seems difficult indeed to get students to devote the same amount of study time or degree of interest to general studies that is usually given to one's A levels. A changing of this requirement would, of course, open up possibilities for the study of a variety of additional courses, possibly including some broad, social science-based offerings.

The growth and development of social studies courses has been hindered in other ways as well. In the Ministry of Education's pamphlet *Citizen's Growing Up*, the importance of preparing young people for the responsibilities of active citizenship is stressed, and headmasters are urged to keep in mind that '*all* education is social education'.[1] (Italics mine.)

This is, of course, a valid point, and one can hardly quarrel with its essential good sense. Yet, taken to extremes (as it often has been here), it leads to a situation in which 'anything goes', in which structure, rigor and organization in syllabus construction are neglected, and in which community service is inadvertently substituted for the systematic study of man and society. *New Society*'s survey (referred to earlier) indicated that many headmasters felt that they *were* offering 'social studies' because their students were visiting old people, helping raise money for a playground, arranging for guest speakers to lecture at the school, etc. To these heads, 'social studies' is *not* perceived as an area of study that draws heavily upon the concepts, generalizations, and methods of the social sciences. It is little wonder, then, given this conception, that the social studies have been widely misunderstood and generally rejected as a serious academic subject.

Naturally enough, then, most of the social studies courses

---

[1] *Citizens Growing Up*, Ministry of Education. Pamphlet No. 16, London: Her Majesty's Stationery Office, 1949. In foreword (unnumbered pages).

that *do* exist are usually found in the curriculum of non-selective secondary schools, and they are more often than not designed for the least able pupils at such schools. This does little to enhance the subject's respectability. Neither does the creation of the Certificate of Secondary Education examination help a great deal, since the C.S.E. was designed for the less academically able. In Cannon's words, 'a subject thus identified with the "non-academic" child has little chance of success in the English education system'.[1]

The case against social studies can be and has been expressed in still other terms. Many English educators fear that courses dealing with more recent history and with current problems of all kinds would lead to political indoctrination of the young. Teachers cannot remain objective (so goes the argument) and therefore it is wiser to postpone discussion of this sort until adulthood. In the meanwhile, the less recent past as well as a physically oriented geography program are obviously safer, less controversial vehicles for the study of man and society.

Similarly, the notion that much of what is suggested for study in social studies courses is in reality unsuited for immature children is prevalent. Hurd, for example, reports a study of (among other things) sixth form masters' reactions to the possibility of teaching sociology to students in the sixteen–eighteen year age bracket. Many thought that grammar school sixth formers were simply not mature enough to deal with this discipline. 'Certain subjects', they said, 'can better be introduced at the later stage of college . . . when the student has a firm training in the basic skills. These subjects . . . demand a certain maturity of judgment and outlook which is lacking in the young.'[2] The Department of Education warns us that we must be careful not to 'carry with us into the classroom matters which are beyond the understanding and fail to arouse the interest of children'.[3] Sound advice, of course, yet it is so interpreted in many places as to rule out the possibility of dealing

<hr>

[1] C. Cannon, 'Social Studies in Secondary Schools', *Educational Review*, Volume 17, No. 1, November 1964, p. 23.

[2] G. E. Hurd, 'Sociology for Sixth Formers?' *Educational Review*, Volume 17, No. 3, p. 210.

[3] *Citizens Growing Up*, Ministry of Education. Pamphlet No. 16, London: Her Majesty's Stationery Office, 1949, p. 23.

in any way with recent history or current controversy. (In the meanwhile, of course, life goes on unmindful of the Department's warnings, and children are constantly exposed to ideas, attitudes, values and events in a manner far less objective than we might expect in the institution society created precisely for the study of such affairs.)

Until now I have attempted to discuss existing hostility to the social studies idea in more or less general terms, and the difficulties enumerated have been attributed to a variety of sources. The geographers and historians, however, have objected far more fully and perhaps more precisely, and a summary of their arguments deserves, perhaps, a separate treatment.

Let us begin with the historians. W. H. Burston of the University of London is certainly one of the most outspoken critics of social studies as a school subject, as well as one of the most articulate. His arguments may be summarized as follows:

1. There is no point in studying current or recent affairs. We can't really find out what society is like today. We need *time* to examine the recent past with historical perspective. Therefore, it is futile to educate people to live in 'contemporary' society; for there are too many versions of what society *is* in reality.

2. Similarly, our own biases make it impossible to study the present in any objective way. We are simply too much a part of it.

3. Knowledge is *not* 'practical experience'. Syllabuses based upon the local and the current programs which enable children to 'come to grips with things by personal experience' rest on false assumptions about the nature of knowledge.

Burston is not averse to setting up straw men, e.g., 'Why do advocates of social studies seek to *replace* history with the study of the contemporary?'[1] Nevertheless, his arguments are generally well reasoned, and he surely remains as a major spokesman for maintenance of the separate subjects approach.

Others have expressed the fear that the social studies approach means the loss of the 'unfolding story of men and women and nations . . . and of world-wide movements'. They express concern that the unique contribution of history cannot be

[1] W. H. Burston, *Social Studies and the History Teacher*, The Historical Association, Teaching of History Leaflet No. 15, London, 1962, pp. 16, 17.

preserved unless the 'recognized content and characteristic method of presentation of each subject is preserved'.[1] The present should be handled through a study of the past, they argue, as one moves chronologically through history, and modern institutions such as labor unions should be dealt with in relation to historical studies of medieval guilds.[2]

The geographer's case was presented quite directly in the Council of the Royal Geographical Society's memorandum, *Geography and 'Social Studies' in Schools*. In essence they argue that 'social studies represent an attempt to compress several branches of learning into one. The result is exactly what happens when a lemon is squeezed: the juice is removed, and only the useless rind and fibres remain . . . "social studies" will destroy the value of geography as an important medium of education, and the Education Committee is concerned at its spread in the schools'. To sum up, then, many historians and geographers believe with complete and sincere confidence that an understanding of man and society in either local, national, or international settings can best be undertaken through a study of *their* disciplines.

The Social Studies and Social Sciences in the 1960's

What, then, of the current status of social studies and social science in English education? Without launching into a detailed *qualitative* analysis, it might be useful simply to examine what *is*—that is, the degree to which such courses are taught in English schools.

To begin with, one should immediately mention the growth of interest in social science in general among English universities. This could be explained in terms of a general recognition that life in a modern, technological society has grown increasingly complex, and that the insights of social science do, after all, offer possible ways of improving the human condition. Undoubtedly the maturation of the social sciences themselves— their vastly improved methodology, their increasingly growing

[1] W. Wallace, 'Some Problems of Teaching Social Studies', *Vocational Aspects*, Volume VI, No. 2, Autumn 1954, p. 141.

[2] *Citizens Growing Up*, Ministry of Education. Pamphlet No. 16, London Her Majesty's Stationery Office, 1949, p. 26.

body of useful concepts and research insights, has had something to do with this upsurge of interest. In any event, all English universities offer degree courses in economics, while sociology is offered at most. Some, such as York and Sussex, allow their students to take combined honors in, say, sociology and politics, sociology and economics, politics and sociology, etc. Sussex and Essex have 'Schools' of Social Studies, and descriptive titles such as 'Indian Civilization', 'Scandinavian Studies', 'European Studies', 'American Studies', 'African, Asian, and South East Asian Studies', 'Social Analysis', etc., appear more and more frequently in university catalogues. Obviously, interdisciplinary, integrated, 'social studies' approaches are catching on, at least at this level of education.

In the colleges of education there is little formal training in social sciences other than sociology. This is not to say that aspects of social science do not reach students in a less structured way, however. Elements of these disciplines find their way into various education courses, and educational psychology is, of course, regularly taught. Educational sociology has become a standard offering at the larger, more influential colleges such as Coventry. Similarly, students are often involved in 'environmental studies'; courses which deal broadly with industry, government, cultural life, etc. On the other hand, 'main course' work in the social sciences in either separate subject or integrated courses was relatively rare, although 'minor' course work was possible at a number of the colleges I visited. (History and geography, as might be expected, were standard main course offerings everywhere.)

The current status of social studies offerings in the primary schools can be summarized in a sentence or two. Except for some exceedingly effective work in local or environmental studies that does go beyond the boundaries of any one discipline, social science and/or social studies simply do not exist. Again, history and geography are more or less standard offerings, and the current wave of reform and interest in the social studies that has so drastically affected American primary education is only beginning to be felt here.

In secondary schools this situation is more complex and, perhaps, more in a state of flux. *New Society* recently conducted a survey of some three thousand secondary schools—independent and maintained, grammar, technical, comprehensive, bilateral and multilateral. Fifty four per cent of the schools responded to their questionnaire (only 36 per cent of the independent schools, incidentally), so that the sample is anything but representative. Similarly, the lack of careful definition of terms led to some confusion among the respondents. Nevertheless, the results seem worth considering here.

To begin with, in answer to the question, 'Do you devote regular periods to social studies?' the overwhelming majority answered 'yes'. Only 86 schools indicated no interest at all. On the other hand, when breaking down the replies in terms of each school's definition of social studies, we find that only 74 were, in fact, offering truly integrated 'social studies' courses. The rest were dealing with social studies topics through the medium of current affairs, general studies, civics, religious instruction, traditional history and geography, liberal studies, independent 'topics', etc.

As is often the case, there seemed to be considerable interest in many of the *topics* and *problems* that might be approached through an organized, explicit course or series of courses. Nevertheless, the respondents indicated that, for the most part, these topics were handled in either peripheral, informal courses or activities with little relationship to the social sciences as scholarly disciplines, or, through traditional offerings in history and geography.[1] It is interesting to note, incidentally, that in Northern England substantial numbers of students take the Northern Universities Joint Matriculation Board's A level examination in 'General Studies'. This examination tends to give considerable emphasis to questions that should, ordinarily, fall under the 'social studies' heading. Apparently, one tries to avoid the *term* 'social studies' even when one does not necessarily avoid the topics themselves that might logically be taught under that heading.

Social studies/social science offering in secondary schools for the G.C.E. are few, indeed. The result of Hurd's study of the sixth form indicated that over 70 per cent of the schools taught *none* of the social sciences to G.C.E. level. British Constitution and Sociology were offered in a few schools, while economics

[1] 'School Social Studies', *New Society*, 3rd September 1964, Volume 4, No. 101, pp. 3–4.

was regularly taught in 22 per cent of the schools—indicating that this discipline has become increasingly popular. It is, in fact, something of a social science island in a sea of more traditional and accepted curricular possibilities.[1] (A recent study carried out at Birmingham University reveals that the systematic study of economics has increased from 1,593 O level and 1,181 A level candidates in 1951 (the first year of the economics G.C.E.) to 9,519 and 9,938 in 1963. No major subject in the secondary curriculum can boast an expansion of this magnitude.[2])

The *New Society* survey referred to earlier summarized the Social Science G.C.E. situation among the 1,500 or so secondary schools they polled as follows:

Schools Offering Social Studies for G.C.E.[3]

	O Level	A Level
Economics	119	376
Law and Government	33	88
Anthropology	—	1
Sociology	1	2
General Studies	117	264
Logic	4	5
Statistics	44	64
Philosophy	1	1
Government	34	70

None of the surveys referred to above deal with social studies offerings in secondary modern schools. The Newsom Report does, however, give us some idea of the relative status of social studies in particular and of the humanities in general in the period prior to the report's publication in 1963. The fourth year curriculum for a 'typical' secondary modern school, according to Newsom, is divided as follows:[4]

[1] G. E. Hurd, 'Sociology for Sixth Formers?' *Educational Review*, Volume 17, No. 3, June 1965, p. 199.

[2] C. D. Harbury and R. Szreter, 'Should Economics be Taught at School?' *New Education*, July 1965, p. 32.

[3] *New Society*, p. 4.

[4] *Half Our Future*, Report of the Central Advisory Council For Education. London: Her Majesty's Stationery Office, 1963, p. 237.

Humanities 39%		*Science & Maths* 24%		*Practical Subjects* 37%	
English	20%	Science	6%	Art & Music	9%
Religious Ed.	6%	Maths	18%	Physical Ed.	10%
History	6%			Wood & Metal Work	12%
Geography	6%			Technical Drawing	6%
Miscellaneous	1%				

My own experience visiting such schools in England indicates that a fairly large percentage—perhaps as many as one quarter—are either now offering or planning social studies courses of some kind for at least their lower streams. (This reflects again, of course, the attitude that 'social studies' is essentially a subject for children of low academic ability.)

The Newsom Report has given considerable indirect support to the social studies movement in non-selective schools. While not openly advocating 'social studies' in place of history and geography, Newsom suggests in its guidelines a series of goals, problems, and examples that seem to call for a broader approach to the study of man and society. For example, the Report suggests the need for a greater emphasis on modern times (1940 to the present); for a greater understanding of others; for a more realistic appraisal of Britain's place in the modern world; for more group work, the use of many educational media, and for greater emphasis on world problems.[1] Newsom concludes that: 'Civics, current affairs, modern history and social studies—whether under these names or not—ought to feature in the programme.'[2] While the Report makes no mention of the possible contributions of social sciences such as sociology, anthropology, political science, and economics (a serious weakness, in my view) it nonetheless does offer considerable encouragement to teachers and heads in non-selective schools who might want to break new ground in these areas.

This attitude is, perhaps, reflected in the considerable interest in the new Certificate of Secondary Education syllabuses in social studies.

[1] Ibid., pp. 163–9.
[2] Ibid., p. 73.

Current Trends

As indicated above, the new C.S.E. (to be reviewed more fully later) *does* include 'social studies' as well as history and geography among its offerings. While the C.S.E. will have little impact on selective schools, it may eventually bring about considerable change in the curriculum of non-selective and comprehensive schools. Other encouraging developments might be enumerated as follows:

1. The British Sociological Association has given considerable support to the development of A level G.C.E. syllabuses so that sociology may be offered at sixth form. (At this writing the Associated Examining Board plans to offer both O and A level syllabuses in Sociology by 1967 or 1968, and the Oxford Board is currently offering an A level examination.)

2. There is increasing interest in what might be called 'education for world understanding' at all levels, primary school through university. This has been reflected in everything from a greater use of global sources for stories and biographies used in primary schools to conferences dealing with international studies at British universities.[1]

3. The recent and increased interest in social studies at the Department of Education and Science. (The Department has recently employed an inspector for social sciences.)

4. The recent report of the Committee on Social Studies, chaired by Lord Heyworth, indicating that the number of university teachers and of students obtaining honors degrees had increased five-fold since 1940.[2]

5. The rapid growth of the 'General Studies' movement in sixth forms, and the concurrent tendency to give increased attention to aspects of social science in such courses.

6. The recent (1965) organization of an association geared to encouraging the teaching of the social sciences at all levels.[3] The group, with its headquarters at the University of London Institute of Education, consists of a number of dynamic school

---

[1] J. L. Henderson, 'The Academic Discipline of World Order', *The Times Educational Supplement*, 15th April 1966, p. 1131.

[2] *Report of the Committee on Social Studies*. London: Department of Education and Science, 1965.

[3] 'The Association For the Teaching of the Social Sciences.' Current Chairman is Mrs C. Cannon, University of London Institute of Education.

and university educators who are devoted to making young people not only 'literate and numerate' but 'sociate' as well.

7. The organization of the Social Science Research Council under the direction of Michael Young, author of the brilliant, satiric, *The Rise of The Meritocracy*. The council has recently spawned a series of committees, each concerned with one of the social sciences. Among other things, the council is interested in reviewing the state of social science research, in fostering exchange between social scientists, and in improving the status and public image of social science in general.

8. Finally, the interest of both the Nuffield Foundation and the influential Schools Council in the curricular problems that will undoubtedly arise when the school leaving age is increased to sixteen is being reflected in an increased awareness of the possible value of social studies courses. The Council's Working Paper is peppered with comments like the following:

> Schools are in the middle of a great, if unco-ordinated activity (in social studies) and it seems reasonable to suppose that the time is ripe for more deliberately organized development work.[1]

> The view of the curriculum put forward in this paper is . . . holistic. It is suggested that it should possess organic unity, and that the organizing principle most likely to provide a sound basis for development is the study of Man, and of human society. . . .[2]

> It is . . . basic to the ideas put forward in this working paper that some understanding . . . of human nature and conduct, and of the means which men use in developing concepts of value for valued human purposes, takes on greater and greater precedence the older the pupils become.[3]

> It is . . . quite evident that the modern world cannot be understood without impinging upon the field of economics, and that sociology, psychology, and anthropology have a contribution to make to a teacher's armoury, even though these descriptions are not likely to appear on the pupil's time-table.[4]

---

[1] Working Paper, No. 2. The School's Council, 38 Belgrave Square, London, S.W.1. October 1965, p. 13.

[2] Ibid., p. 12.

[3] Ibid., p. 11.

[4] Ibid., p. 14.

In summary, then, it appears that integrated cross-disciplinary courses in 'social studies' are, perhaps, to have a 'second chance' in English education. Whether or not this movement succeeds will, of course, depend upon the curriculum workers' ability to avoid the pitfalls of the past as well as adequately to gauge the needs of children now and in the decades to follow. Similarly, the availability of adequate financial support for curricular innovation and experimentation will undoubtedly play an equally important role in determining the acceptance or rejection of 'social studies' by the schools.

II: SOCIAL STUDIES IN PRIMARY SCHOOLS

IN GENERAL, primary schools appear to be the particular strength of English education—despite the handicaps of overcrowding, poor physical facilities, teacher shortages, and the always potentially limiting effects of eleven plus selection. At best, primary teachers treat children as individuals, not hesitating to move them into reading, for example, in reception classes if they are *ready*—and, similarly, not pushing children too quickly—perhaps beyond their abilities—as soon as they reach the age of six. Teachers tend to rely more upon their own wit and creativity than they do on commercially prepared work books and exercise sheets, and there is considerable emphasis on freedom of expression in the teaching of art, prose and poetry, music and movement. To illustrate in more specific terms, let me describe my observations in a few of the dozen or so primary schools.

BAMPTON PRIMARY SCHOOL

Bampton is an Oxfordshire school of about 200 children. It can best be described as rural, although the building itself is attractively new. As we approach it we see a group of seven- or eight-year-old boys working outdoors on a carpentry table, protected from the elements by an overhanging roof. As we move indoors, we are impressed immediately with the evidence of the prodigious efforts in arts and crafts that surround us. Paintings, drawings, modelling, weaving and block prints are attractively displayed everywhere, and the school seems full of busy, contented, *responsible* children.

One group of nine-year-olds is making booklets describing a visit to Goldsmith's College in London, where they stayed for a week in a college residence hall. They used this as a base of operations for trips to the Tower of London, Greenwich Park (they were particularly interested in its astronomical clock) and other points of interest in London.

Another group had made a trip to Blenheim Palace, and their attractive drawings and booklets were already on display —including written descriptions of the palace and gardens, brass rubbings, etc.

Another class of eight- and nine-year-olds has just completed a study or 'topic' on the American Indians. The teacher feels the important thing is that the children will be interested enough in Indians to want to read and write about them, as well as plan art or crafts projects related to Indians. The topic itself doesn't matter, I am told—it's merely a way of getting children interested and active.

A class of ten- and eleven-year-olds had studied 'prehistoric times'. They visited 'White Horse Hill' where they looked for bones and other relics, did 'soil augering', found some tiles from an ancient cottage, made maps of their route, and wrote separate reports on 'Wheels', 'A Bronze-age village', 'Farming in the Bronze Age', etc.

All of the work described above took place in the junior school. There was no evidence of formal social studies activities in the infant classrooms.

TOWER HILL PRIMARY SCHOOL

Again in Oxfordshire, and again a relatively new, attractive building. The children come largely from lower middle class backgrounds and there are few if any with 'professional' parents. Eleven plus selection still exists in Oxfordshire, but this has little effect on Tower Hill School. Education goes on unperturbed, and about the same number pass as do in the rest of the county. In all the classrooms I visited, children were working independently and purposefully as individuals or in small groups. The walls were covered here, as they were in Bampton School, with beautiful paintings, drawings, and other samples of children's creative endeavors. A teacher of a 'family group' of five-, six-, and seven-year-olds had just returned from a holiday in Holland, and she had shown her children photographs, Dutch money, and other items of interest.

Everywhere teachers made use of the real, the concrete—of *things* of all kinds. An art lesson was going on during which children were comparing a simple pottery jug with an elaborate silver chalice; another group was drawing a *real* pheasant's head, while a third group was sketching an exquisite display of wine bottles of all shapes and sizes.

Another class had studied the origins of the woollen industry in the Cotswolds, and had managed to obtain a huge nineteenth-century weaving machine (set up in the school's multipurpose room) for study. On the basis of a series of field trips to woollen mills, sheep farms, etc., the class eventually created a series of beautifully illustrated 'history' booklets about the woollen industry and its origins.

Talks with the headmaster and his staff revealed that there is no formal social studies curriculum or syllabus. Topics are studied that are of interest to the children—sometimes as a class, but more often as small groups. The total atmosphere of the school is intended to contribute to social education, and much attention is given to the assuming of responsibility by children, pupil-teacher planning, help projects for the elderly, etc.

GILLESPIE PRIMARY SCHOOL

In contrast to the two Oxfordshire schools described above, Gillespie School is located in the heart of London, in a working class area surrounded by old houses that have been split up into a number of apartments. There has been a considerable influx of immigrants, and reciprocally, an outflow of the area's original, largely Anglo-Saxon population. About half of the 400 children in the school are English; the rest are divided among Greek and Turkish Cypriots, West Indians, Italians, French-speaking Moroccans, Indians and Pakistanis, and West Africans.

Every immigrant child that enters Gillsepie School is given a careful, individual, diagnostic analysis, and then is assigned to a regular classroom. Depending upon his specific problems and needs, each immigrant child will be assigned to special classes with one or two helping teachers that are part of the school's permanent staff.

The headmaster has put together a broad history-geography syllabus which allows a great deal of selection by teachers.

From the age of seven on up, however, children *are* expected to deal with social studies topics, and there was evidence throughout the school that this was, in fact, taking place. Current events topic books were everywhere in evidence, although a number of the teachers perceived the essential purpose or value of such activities as providing 'interesting subjects for the children to write about'. In the more formal teaching of history and geography, the project method was used, i.e., the teacher gave some sort of general introduction, the children divided up into interest groups of five or six each, and the study was carried out by such groups under the guidance of the teacher. The feeling was strongly expressed (by the headmaster *and* his staff) that children are very much interested in the world in general—that purely 'local' or environmental studies could often become a bore, and that children *can* learn vicariously. A group of seven-year-olds, then, had just completed a simple study of China, based largely on pictorial materials and children's books obtained by the teacher. The children organized their ideas in a large, beautifully illustrated 'class book'. As one walks through the halls and classrooms one finds that the walls are covered with paintings and murals of all kinds—each a product of a given class's study of the world and people that surround them. Because of the headmaster's diligence, funds have been obtained to take children on a great variety of field trips and excursions—including visits to Hampton Court, the British Museum, Stratford, Canterbury, London Airport, Windsor Castle, Portsmouth and Southampton, two-week visits to the Isle of Wight, and even a trip to Belgium.

MEDBOURNE PRIMARY SCHOOL

This is a tiny village school in Leicestershire—two teachers and about 45 children, both infants and juniors. In many ways the school resembles those in Oxfordshire. Carpentry, 'straw' and clay modeling, painting and weaving are obviously important activities, and a good deal of each school day is given over to relatively free, unstructured studies and activities. Since there is no eleven plus selection here (Leicestershire has adopted a comprehensive system of secondary education) no particular curriculum pressure is exerted from this source. Neither does the local education authority exert any compelling curricular demands, and so the two teachers are free to develop the kind of program they feel is appropriate for their boys and girls.

The juniors had just completed a study of an 'imaginary country'. They located it on the globe, made a large model of it in clay, gave it certain physical features, and created an imaginary history of its settlement. They did not, however, examine the possible relationship between location, physical features, and climate. Nor did they consider the sorts of problems involved in the settlement of a 'new country'—the need for some form of government, for example. Its chief value, I was told, was as a motivational exercise for creative writing and art.

The juniors at Medbourne also carried out a local study centering on a 'village survey'. They found out where the people who settled in the village came from, and recorded the varying places of origin on a large map. They studied the village's history and growth, where people work, how the land is used, where the main buildings are located, the services provided in the village, and the duties of the Parish Council. They tape recorded a number of interviews with older inhabitants, and studied the way the village had changed over time. Railroad growth was charted, for example, as were the development of highways and bus-lines.

The village survey took approximately three months to complete, and (along with the 'imaginary country' project described above) represented the formal work in social studies planned for that academic year.

These, then, were obviously good schools—impressive schools —schools that were, in many ways, meeting the specific educational needs of particular groups of children, and schools in which modern, effective educational practices were carried out in almost every aspect of the curriculum. All of the primary schools I visited could not, of course, be so described. I think of one, for example, in which the teacher of a class of nine-year-olds copied factual statements from his own notebook on to the blackboard, and the children dutifully copied this material into notebooks of their own. This was followed by a flash card drill consisting of a series of questions on (I presume) yesterday's copying.

Nevertheless, the schools I have described in some detail—and particularly those in Oxfordshire and Leicestershire—*do* represent the best in English primary education. This is not merely the opinion of a foreign observer—rather, it is, in general, the opinion of primary education leaders everywhere, including Her Majesty's Inspectors at the Department of Education and Science, Education faculty members at University Institutes and Departments of Education and at Colleges of Education, influential school administrators such as Sir Alec Clegg of West Riding, and forward-looking teachers and headmasters. The primary schools of Oxfordshire, Leicestershire, West Riding, Hertfordshire and some other areas represent, in general, the ideal in English primary education as perceived by those in positions of educational authority and leadership in England, and an understanding of the philosophy and practices that dominate them gives one insight into the direction in which English primary education, in general, appears to be moving, as well as some understanding of the role played by social studies in such schools.

It might be useful at this point to turn from eye-witness descriptions of classroom activities to an examination of the curriculum guides or syllabuses that represent the more formal efforts of headmasters and (occasionally) teachers to organize programs of study in environmental studies, or more traditional courses in history and geography .While the following syllabuses are neither the best (nor the worst) that I have seen, they are fairly representative of the sort of guidelines one is likely to encounter.

SCHEME OF WORK IN ENVIRONMENTAL STUDIES[1]

1. WHAT IS MEANT BY THE ENVIRONMENT?
   (a) *The immediate environment:* the child's immediate surrounding. These include the school, the classroom, the home, people, parents and friends, the teacher.

---

[1] Excerpts taken from the Mornington Road School Syllabus, Bingley, West Riding, Yorkshire.

(*b*) *The wider environment:* not under immediate control and and therefore generally accepted as being factors which influence the way of life in the district in which the child lives and in which the school is set. It comprises:

1. *Natural and physical features:* rivers, hills, valleys, woods, types of terrain, soils.
2. *Flora and fauna:* existing as an effect of No. 1, but not always obviously so.
3. *Man's use of his environment:* his organization of and attempts to control it, farming, industries, transport systems (road, rail, water, air).
4. *The environment's control of man:* weather patterns and the effect of types of terrain on industry. The existence of needs for services and how man has supplied those services. Types of home, building materials (e.g., Why are most homes in Bingley except new ones, built of stone, not brick?)
5. *The environment as an introduction to other places:* comparisons with other regions of England and (in the older classes) with other parts of the world.

2. PLANNING

Since children of different ages will extract different points of value from the same experience, there is no need to save some parts of the environment for later work.

3. WHAT IS TO BE LEARNED?

Naturally there will be a fusion of all traditional 'subjects' that are concerned with relationships. Nature study, Geography, History, Science, Mathematics (as distinct from 'sums') will all be learned. There should be a growth of personal bonds with the environment. The bright child will be able to see the interesting way some societies are built up and how our lives are constructed within our civilization. It might be hoped too that through these methods of observation, inquiry, analysis, and expression, ways of thinking might be developed. The growth of language is involved here. A word is a label. *Understanding of words depends on first-hand experience.*

4. HOW IS IT TO BE LEARNED?

By actual experience . . . GOING OUT, going and looking about or going to specifically see something. There is NO substitute for first-hand experience. Not even TV.

By following up an interest. Sometimes an interest will arise naturally and individually. The teacher may point out items of interest but cannot often create it. Teacher should not dominate nor be disappointed if the children do not share her interests. Permit the experience to be wide enough to allow for personal differences. Teacher should join interested groups, help them to see, stimulate their interest once it has been aroused. DON'T GET IN THE WAY.

HISTORY[1]

INFANTS

Ideas of time mean very little at this stage. History, or rather 'Once upon a time long before we were born . . .' should be introduced by way of a well-told or well-read story. This will stimulate the imagination and arouse an interest in times long past of strange people and customs. Stories of the Ancient World, Egypt, Babylon, China, Greece, for example, will provide a wide field of legend, myth, and fact to choose from. Some of the well-known legends of Europe should also be recounted, e.g. the Norse Tales.

JUNIORS

First Year
The early work of the first year should be a continuation of the work outlined above with increasing concern for ways of living, dress, transport, etc. The remainder of the year will cover the period in Britain from prehistoric man to the Vikings.

Second Year
The Conquest to the Wars of the Roses.

Third Year
The Tudors and Stuarts.

Fourth Year
The Georgians to the Present Day.

The sequence of time is difficult for the young to comprehend, but appreciation should develop throughout the school so that by the fourth year the concept should be emerging. It is helpful if comparisons are drawn with the ages of their parents and

---

[1] Excerpts taken from the Gillespie Primary School Syllabus, London.

grandparents and so on. Tudor times may be regarded, for example, as being about 400 years ago. Although this is only approximate it serves as a landmark to which references can be made when necessary. From this questions may arise as to dates. The teacher's approach and the degree of correlation with other activities, when each year's work is planned, is a matter of personal choice. The period may be studied from the point of view of the development of building techniques, changes in dress, improvements in transport, famous people or outstanding events. There may be a selection of such topics chosen for study, or they may all be undertaken, with additions, by a class divided into groups.

GEOGRAPHY[1]

INFANTS

At this stage children are exploring their environment and much that they are interested in could be considered as Geography or Science. Therefore the framework of suggestions below is applicable to both.

The children's love of collecting all kinds of things should be encouraged and utilized by the teacher. Let the collection develop beyond the leaves, flowers and pond life of the Nature Table. Samples of earth, stone and metal provide useful material for observation and discussions. Likewise do mechanical objects, batteries, wire and bulbs, toy telescopes and binoculars, compasses and magnets.

Such an approach through children's own interests should evoke a lively response, a desire to find out more, and some purposeful activity in observations, simple records, art and craft. Visits to local parks should prove helpful at all times.

JUNIORS

The children are still exploring their environment, but have a greater store of knowledge and experience and a desire to know about the world in general. They want to learn about people in other lands, what they grow or make, how they live, the weather, the countryside. Also, they become interested in what things are made of, i.e. the raw materials of industry and the food they eat.

The aim of approach are numerous, but account should be taken of what is interesting, familiar, and near at hand, and also,

---

[1] Excerpts taken from the Gillespie Primary School Syllabus, London.

obviously vary. The unfamiliar requires either well-told first-hand knowledge or reading from carefully selected materials which supply interesting details. It is suggested that several books be used when a topic is studied in order that there shall be in the classroom varied information and illustrations. Map work should play an important part in the work throughout the school by frequent use of atlases and the globe.

The scheme of work outlined below is not meant to be exhaustive; it is hoped that teachers will interpret it imaginatively, extend where necessary and produce a lively and varied response from the children in related fields.

1st Year

Maps. What a map is—a looking down view. Establish by making maps of objects in the class, e.g. the desk. Then maps of the room, etc.; the school and surrounding streets; maps of how to get to school; land and sea on the globe.
Britain. The farmer and his animals. What they eat, how they are cared for, their uses.
The World. Animals in other lands.

2nd Year

Maps—direction; the shape of Great Britain; why are some maps coloured? Map of a local shopping area.
Britain. Local—survey of shops and their products. Select and study some that are made or grown in Britain, e.g. woollen goods, wheat.
The World. Products from other countries, e.g. cocoa, rubber.

3rd Year

Maps. Map colours—the high and lowland of Great Britain. The railway network spreading from London; rivers. Sea and air routes.
Britain. Local factories. What do they make. Other men at work, e.g. fishermen, coal-miners.
The World. Work in other lands, e.g. oil, lumbering.

4th Year

Maps. Distances on a map. Some map symbols.
Britain. Contrast of weather, e.g. Wales and East Anglia. Its effect on soil, crops, and animals.
The World. Contrast of climate, e.g. Equitoral and Tundra lands. Its effect on soil, crops, and animals.

Before turning to some general questions, criticisms, and comments, let us consider the purposes and rationale of primary school history and geography programs in more detail, since (despite the trends toward integrated local and environmental studies described earlier) these disciplines are still taught as separate subjects in many English primary schools.

In general, it would be difficult to quarrel with the broad overall objective of history teaching in the primary schools that appears in references such as the Department of Education and Science's *Teaching History*. The two essential purposes are described as follows:

> . . . One is the moral motive, the view that it is good for boys' and girls' character that they should hear or read about great men and women of the past and so learn gradually to discriminate between disinterested and selfish purposes, or between heroism and cowardice. And the other is the motive that they should be introduced to their heritage, introduced, that is, to the way things have come about, and so to their own environment, in which they will have to live and to act. . . .[1]

To these underlying purposes, the authors add two more: the development of imaginative experience and the awakening of curiosity.[2] Other apparently well-accepted assumptions that might be worthy of considerably more debate, however, also appear regularly in the literature dealing with the teaching of history to relatively young children. For example:

> The syllabuses . . . must *always* be based on the clear assumption that children of junior age are not logically minded, that they are not capable of sustained attention, that their attention is of the sensuous and not of the intellectual type, and that it can, therefore, be successfully directed only to objects and not to ideas and beliefs.[3] [Italics mine.]

> The syllabus will avoid any hint of the inculcation of 'inert ideas'. Among these . . . are the principles of political and social changes, religious revolutions, and all that we may bring broadly under

---

[1] *Teaching History*, Ministry of Education. Pamphlet No. 23, London: Her Majesty's Stationery Office, 1952.

[2] Ibid., p. 19.

[3] C. F. String, *History in the Primary School*. London: University of London Press Ltd, 1964, p. 99.

the heading of cause and effect, since these ideas have meaning only at a much later stage of development.[1]

The background of (a) document, who wrote it, why it was written . . . all of these questions, and many others . . . are generally beyond the abilities . . . of a pupil in the junior or middle school.[2]

It would be equally difficult to disagree with the overall goals of geography as set forth in the Department of Education and Science's booklet, *Geography and Education*. For example:

It seems then, that children need scope for their curiosity, their sense of wonder, their feeling for beauty, and their delight in stories of courage and adventure. It seems also that, in the field of geography, opportunities for satisfying these needs can be provided both by what the children experience round their own school and home and also by what they learn of other parts of the world. Geography at this stage, then, is concerned with both the immediate and with the world beyond.[3]

. . . some knowledge is appropriate to whole groups or classes . . . major distributions of land and sea, major international events and the main strands of our Christian heritage, will probably be common to juniors throughout the land. The teacher, though not confined to a rigid syllabus, will have in mind what is valuable in our local and national story and also a picture of the kind of world geography toward which each of his pupils will move. . . .[4]

Similarly, those statements concerning the nature of geography as a school subject seem to me to be particularly well conceived. For example:

Geography maintains the need for looking at things as a whole and it is in his regional method that the geographer makes his unique contribution to learning.[5]

All spatial phenomena, including cultural ones, come within the purview of regional geography. Those selected for emphasis in a

---

[1] Ibid., p. 100.

[2] *The Teaching of History*. The Incorporated Association of Assistant Masters in Secondary Schools. Cambridge: Cambridge University Press, 1965, p. 45.

[3] *Geography and Education*, Ministry of Education. Pamphlet No. 39, London: Her Majesty's Stationery Office, 1962, p. 15.

[4] Ibid., p. 18.

[5] Ibid., p. 17.

given regional study will be those considered significant . . . for the delineation of the region's character.[1]

> There is . . . an 'order of reality' in regional study: first the study of a small region in the field. Then the study of small regions of comparable area through material which is as nearly first hand as possible, and then the study of larger and larger regions. . . .[2]

Other statements, however, are open to considerably more debate. For example:

> . . . there is a case to be made out for dropping part of the orthodox syllabus of regional teaching and leaving this type of work until the third year (of secondary school). *Starting then at an age when children . . . have developed intellectually to a point where they can appreciate the import of regional geography* a course can be planned leading up to the O Level certificate.[3] [Italics mine.]

> We should not be afraid to say to our pupils that we are going to . . . reject much that they have been taught as truth at an earlier stage . . . we shall have done them no service if our teaching has not prepared them to throw away some of their *carefully nurtured* earlier beliefs.[4] [Italics mine.]

> Not until they are about nine years old do children possess the necessary capacity for accurate imagination.[5]

Primary School Social Studies—An Evaluation

Until now I have largely attempted to describe what *is*, rather than react to the practices and statements outlined above in any critical manner. At this point, then, it might be useful to attempt a more critical analysis of the teaching of social studies in state-supported English primary schools.

No one who had given any serious effort to the study of primary education here can possibly underemphasize the influence of Piaget. We find evidence of this in every aspect of the primary school curriculum, and particularly, in the social studies. Many of the practices described above are traceable to him, as are some of the quoted statements relating to

---

[1] Ibid., p. 7.

[2] Ibid., p. 8.

[3] R. C. Chorley and P. Haggett, Editors. *Frontiers in Geographical Teaching*. London: Methuen and Company, Ltd, 1965, p. 330.

[4] Ibid., p. 332.

[5] *Teaching Geography in Junior Schools*. Sheffield: The Geographical Association, 1959, p. 7.

educational goals and procedures.

Without attempting anything approaching a complete treatment of Piaget's work, it might be useful to list at least a few of his pertinent conclusions—more, perhaps, as a reminder than as a summary.

The reader will undoubtedly recall Piaget's findings concerning the egocentricity of children's thinking under the age of seven or eight—their tendency to approach problem situations largely in terms of their own, personal (and of course, limited) problem solving strategies which seldom include a step-by-step, reasoned analysis. What *he* (i.e., the child) thinks is probably correct, and he is unaware that others may approach a solution differently. Children at this age have great difficulty in providing causal explanations of a variety of phenomena. Similarly, attempts to either objectively understand or communicate with others are rare below the age of seven or eight. There is little tendency for children at this age to ask 'why' questions, and 'logical' explanations are seldom asked or given. It is difficult, before the age of eleven or twelve, to make logical judgments about the ideas or beliefs of others, or to be aware of relationships.

Piaget's contributions to our understanding of children and childhood are, of course, educational landmarks of our time. In a larger sense, his position as an educational researcher, a pioneer, indeed as a giant among ordinary men is secure. Yet Piaget himself continues to probe further, to ask new questions, to re-shape old ones, and to refine techniques. The body of research related to children's thinking continues to grow, and others, too, have made significant contributions—many of which do not support Piaget's conclusions. One thinks immediately, for example, of Kenneth Wann's study, *Fostering the Intellectual Development of Young Children*,[1] carried out at Teachers' College, Columbia; or of Dorothy Lee's fascinating cross-cultural study of the education of the shtetl Jews of Eastern Europe,[2] which apparently cannot be explained in terms of

---

[1] K. Wann and Associates, *Fostering the Intelligent Development of Young Children*. New York:

[2] Dorothy Lee, 'Developing the Drive to Learn and the Questioning Mind' *Freeing Capacity to Learn*. Association for Supervision and Curriculum Development, Washington, D.C.

Piaget's conceptions about reasoning in children. The work of Bruner, Taba, Hazlitt, Suchman, Grener and Rath, Bloom, Fahe, Broun, Bloom and Broder, Deutsche, McAndrew, Torrance[1] and others raises additional questions that might at least, encourage a degree of continued open-mindedness about the educational problems Piaget has (and is) considering.

David Russell, in his important work, *Children's Thinking*, summarized some of the current criticisms of Piaget as follows:

1. Most of Piaget's records are obtained in one type of rather peculiar play situation, with children in pairs in a free school situation, and in interviews with one adult. Different results might be obtained in Geneva and have been obtained in other countries in situations where children are members of groups of four or six years.

2. Piaget does not agree with other writers in his definitions of terms. Some of his examples do not seem to fit his definitions. His definition of reasoning, for instance, makes reasoning a highly theoretical verbal process rather than the somewhat

---

[1] J. Bruner, J. Goodnow, and G. A. Austin, *A Study of Thinking*. New York: Wiley, 1956; H. Taba, 'Thought Processes and Teaching Strategies in Elementary Social Studies', Paper presented to the American Education Research Association, Chicago, 17th February 1962; V. Hazlitt, 'Children's Thinking', *British Journal of Psychology*, Volume 20, 1930, pp. 354–61. See also D. Layton, 'An Exploratory Study of Primary Grade Children's Ability to Conceptualize Based Upon Content Drawn from Selected Social Studies Topics', unpublished master's thesis, The University of Minnesota, Minneapolis, 1964; R. Suchman, The Elementary School Training Program in Scientific Inquiry, mimeographed, Urbana: University of Illinois, 1962; N. Grener and L. E. Raths, 'Thinking in Grade VI', *Educational Research Bulletin*, Ohio State University, Volume 24, 1945; B. S. Bloom, 'Some Results of a Study of Conscious Thought Processes in Classroom Situations', *American Psychologist*, Volume, 6, 1951; G. L. Fahe, 'The Questioning Activity of Children', *Journal of Genetic Psychology*, Volume 60, 1942; C. T. Broun, 'An Experimental Diagnosis of Thinking on Controversial Issues', *Speech Monograph*, Volume 17, 1950; B. S. Bloom and L. J. Broder, *Problem Solving Processes of College Students*, Supplementary Educational Monographs, No. 73, Chicago: University of Chicago Press, 1950; J. M. Deutsche, 'The Development of Children's Concepts of Causal Relations', *The University of Minnesota Institute of Child Welfare Monograph*, No. 13, 1937; M. B. McAndrew, 'An Experimental Investigation of Young Children's Ideas of Causality', *Studies of Psychology and Psychiatry: Catholic University of America*, Volume 6, 1943, No. 2; P. Torrance, 'Current Research in the Nature of Creative Talent', *Journal of Counseling Psychology*, Volume 6, 1959, pp. 309–16.

simpler problem-solving process it appeared to be in many other experiments.

3. Some of Piaget's findings and hypotheses are based on small groups of children rather than on a variety of types from different backgrounds.

4. Piaget's work shows almost complete disregard for the use of experimental controls and does not utilize any of the scientific methods of child study such as time-sampling techniques or other tests of observations developed in the United States and Britain.

5. Piaget not only omits some of the usual precautions in sampling and in scientific controls; he also avoids any statistical treatment of his data. He often quotes freely from his protocols but gives no indication of such data as frequency, reliability of differences at various age levels, etc.

6. Many studies have found evidence of reasoning ability in children as early as three or four years of age. As suggested above, this may be due to variations in the definition of reasoning.

7. Piaget fails to stress the wide difference among individual children in languages, concepts, and problem-solving abilities.

8. Piaget overstresses the importance of stages in thinking, particularly in making rather distinct breaks at an age of about seven years in egocentric versus social language and at eleven years in prelogical thinking versus reasoning.[1]

None of this means that Piaget's work should be completely ignored in favor of some new conception—but it should, at least, encourage a more cautious approach to it.

Our first basic point, then, is that Piaget's findings—as interpreted here—seem to have had an undue influence on aspects of primary school social studies education in England; an influence often leading to overtly simplistic, intellectually undemanding studies emphasizing the 'concrete', and (therefore) the nearby, while consistently putting off more challenging approaches that might begin to develop more complex thinking strategies and studies at much earlier age levels.

A second, somewhat related point concerns the tendency in English primary schools largely to ignore (in social studies programs) the results of a growing body of research dealing

---

[1] D. Russell, *Children's Thinking*. New York: Ginn and Company, 1956, pp. 160–1.

with the development of attitudes, values, prejudices and stereotypes in young children. One American researcher, for example, has summarized some of the more striking conclusions that seem to have emerged from a host of studies dealing with the development of and causes of prejudice in children. Among her findings are the following:

1. Inter-group prejudice in children makes its appearance at an early age—sometimes in children as young as four. [These findings are in direct conflict with the view commonly held among many teachers I talked with here, i.e. that negative feelings toward particular groups do not arise until or shortly before adolescence.]
2. Apparently, these studies tend to support the conclusion that segregation, prejudice, discrimination and their social concomitants potentially damage the personalities of *all* children —those in the majority as well as those in the minority.
3. Experimental programs such as the Philadelphia Early Childhood Project and others indicate that specific activities in schools can help to diminish or even reverse racial and other prejudices.[1]

Similarly, the research of Merriam, Turner, Easton and Hess, and others dealing with the political socialization of the young indicates that political attitudes and values develop (whether teachers like it or not) during the primary school years. Apparently a vast array of factors (from television to the casual comments of a school bus driver) influence and contribute to the development of such values.[2]

Now, none of this suggests that racial problems in England approach the severity of these in the U.S. (although they are growing) or, that if these studies were replicated here, similar results would occur. Nevertheless, they *do* suggest that the primary school years are a truly crucial educational period in a child's life—a period during which formal education *could*

[1] R. Arter, 'The Effects of Prejudice on Children', *Children*, September–October, 1959.

[2] C. E. Merrian, *The Making of Citizens: A Comparative Study of Methods of Civic Training*. Chicago: University of Chicago Press, 1931.

M. E. Turner, *The Child Within the Group: An Experiment in Self-Government.* Stanford, California: Stanford University Press, 1957.

D. Easton and R. Hess, 'The Child's Political World', *The Midwest Journal of Political Science*, Fall, 1962.

consciously begin to counter-attack many of the negative influences that affect children's lives. Attitudes and values *are* being formed—some of them based on fair and honest answers to children's questions given by perceptive and sensitive parents, others based on the worst kind of rumor and gossip. The schools, and in particular, the social studies, exist as a possible vehicle for reasoned and objective exploration of the child's wider world—whether or not they will be utilized more effectively for this purpose remains to be seen.

A third criticism relates essentially to conceptions of the nature of the content or subject matter to be studied. My experiences in English primary schools have led me to the conclusion that curriculum workers here generally view curricular problems in one of two extreme positions. The first view (and the more traditional and less accepted position) is simply that there are certain topics, certain periods in history, certain places on the Earth's surface, certain facts that people need to 'know'. The curriculum is so structured as to include coverage of these facts and topics. Curricular revision generally involves arguments concerning whether or not we are spending too much time with the Tudors and Stuarts, whether we ought to give increased attention to Commonwealth countries, etc., and a 'revised' syllabus often results in a mere re-shuffling of quite similar topics, periods and places.

The second view is largely a violent reaction against the first. I think, perhaps, it is expressed most vividly by an American writer, John Holt, writing in his controversial, *How Childern Fail:*

> We cannot have real learning in school if we think it is our duty and our right to tell children what they must learn. We cannot know, at any moment, what particular bits of knowledge or understanding a child needs most, will most strengthen and best fit his model of reality. Only he can do this. He may not do it very well, but he can do it a hundred times better than we can. The most we can do is to try to help, by letting him know roughly what is available and where he can look for it. Choosing what he wants to learn and what he does not is something he must do for himself.[1]

---

[1] J. Holt, *How Children Fail.* New York: Pitman Publishing Corp., 1964, p. 179.

I would suggest that there is a third way—an approach that allows for a great deal of leeway in the selection of specific content to be studied, yet provides at the same time a curriculum focused on fundamental social science concepts and generalizations that may facilitate transfer, cut down on the factual, topical syllabus load, and still be appropriate in developmental terms for relatively young children.

Without dwelling on the details of the curricular revolution which is currently sweeping American social studies education,[1] a few comments by Jerome Bruner might serve to clarify this alternative for English readers. Since Bruner is directing the Elementary Social Studies Project of Educational Services Incorporated (now known as the Educational Development Center, or E.D.C.), it may be particularly helpful to quote liberally from his writing in *Man: A Course of Study*—a working paper setting forth some guidelines for E.S.I.'s elementary school social studies syllabus:

> We begin . . . with an account of the substance or structure of a course in 'social studies' now in the process of construction. . . . The content of the course is man: his nature as a species, the forces that shaped and continue to shape his humanity. Three questions recur throughout:
>
> > What is human about human beings?
> > How did they get that way?
> > How can they be made more so?
>
> In pursuit of our questions we shall explore five matters, each closely associated with the evolution of man as a species, each defining at once the distinctiveness of man and his potentiality for further evolution. The five great humanizing forces are, of course, tool-making, language, social organization, the management of man's prolonged childhood, and man's urge to explain. . . .[2]

Quite obviously, one might explore some of Bruner's 'essential questions' through a great variety of content. This type of

[1] See *Social Education*, April 1965, for a summary of these developments, or chapter eight in the Association for Supervision and Curricular Development's *New Curriculum Developments*, edited by G. Unruh and available from the Association, 1021 Sixteenth Street, N.W. Washington, D.C.

[2] J. Bruner, *Man: A Course of Study*. Cambridge, Massachusetts: Educational Service, Inc., 1965, pp. 3, 4, 22.

curricular organization leaves the curriculum worker free to choose from among a number of specific illustrations (i.e., 'content') and to select teaching strategies that are most appropriate for his school or his children. On the other hand, Bruner and his colleagues seem to know where they are headed in broad, conceptual terms, and an exposure to the E.S.I. curriculum (whatever its weaknesses) ought to at least insure children against either a social studies program based exclusively upon a devotion to 'facts' and 'coverage' *or* one that is completely laissez-faire. No one suggests that Bruner's approach is necessarily appropriate for English children. Nevertheless, he does offer an alternative curricular conception that ought to be explored in much greater detail in England than it has at this writing.

Fourth (and this seems true whether or not one adopts Brunerian curricular concepts), I would suggest that those concerned with primary education in England have thought too little about the related problems of priorities and sequence in the social studies curriculum. In one school I visited, the children had studied three topics during the last two terms: 'Israel', 'Australia', and 'Trees'. I am not in any sense opposed to trees, nor am I unaware of the related problems of conservation, etc., that could conceivably be brought into such a study. Nevertheless, I would suggest that both 'Israel' and 'Australia' offer far more fruitful possibilities for social studies learning, and to give equal time and attention to all three topics indicated considerable disregard for the social sciences upon which systematic teaching in social studies relies.

I found a number of teachers who questioned this curricular egalitarianism—particularly those who were impressed with the effectiveness of some of the newer syllabuses in maths and science—and the notion that some topics were, after all, of greater significance than others (whether offered in 'environmental studies' or in more conventional programs in history and geography) was obviously bothering a good many individuals.

Similarly, I found teachers concerned with the problems of repetition and unrelatedness. Many felt that no one cared particularly whether or not quite similar topics were studied year in and year out, and still less attention was given to the problem of developing social studies concepts in any ordered, sequential way. This was true, incidentally, despite the often enthusiastic responses of headmasters, L.E.A. inspectors, and others to newer maths programs that quite consciously introduced children to mathematical ideas in an ordered, related manner.

A fifth concern has to do with what seems to be an overemphasis on the near, the local, or if you will, the parochial. Blyth has referred to local studies as 'an opiate of the peasantry', often 'Arcadian and bucolic',[1] in nature, while Ian Lister has referred to local history as 'mere antiquarianism'.[2] Both statements were made with tongue-in-cheek, and both are of course exaggerations. Nevertheless, there does appear to be a tendency to equate all that is good with all that is local in English primary schools, and the local environment is utilized far more as an end in itself rather than as a point of departure for broader studies or as a *known* focal point for comparison with the unknown. Similarly, there is little attempt to use the local environment for more evaluative and perhaps less descriptive, truly *social* studies of local mores, problems, and life-ways that might lead to an understanding of significant ideas related to social behavior and social structure.

Sixth, I would suggest that there are, after all, limits to how far one can go with personal, concrete experience as *the* essential teaching technique. Children can study only a small part of the world by direct observation and experience, and one must question the hours that are spent in making, building, and *physically* 'doing' that could, conceivably, be used in other ways as well. One wonders, for example, if in studying the woollen industry the *process* of making wool does not get treated all out of proportion to some of the related economic, social, and, in fact, even political problems that might be implied in such a study—granting, of course, that much of this 'activity' would be intellectual rather than physical, vicarious more than direct.

Closely related to this criticism is the seeming reluctance of

---

[1] W. A. L. Blyth, *English Primary Education*, Volume II. London: Routledge and Kegan Paul, 1965, p. 101.

[2] J. H. Plumb, Editor, *Crisis in the Humanities*. London: Penguin Books, 1964, p. 167.

teachers and headmasters who are exceedingly creative in fields such as maths to spend much time devising equally creative techniques for improving social studies instruction. Apart from the excellent 'sample studies' developed by geographers, there seems to be little activity in this field. Without launching into a complete description of new media and techniques, it might be of interest to consider, as an example, the fascinating notion of developing a series of 'games' for teaching purposes, as described by Bruner:

> . . . we are now developing a 'family' of games designed to bring social organization into personal consciousness of the children.

> The first of these games, 'hunting', is designed to simulate conditions in an early human group engaged in hunting and is patterned on the life and ecology of the Bushmen of the Kalahari desert. The elements of the game are Hunters, Prey, Weapons, Habitats, Messages, Predators, and Food. Without going into detail, the game simulates (in the manner of so-called Pentagon games used for increasing the sensitivities of generals) the problem of planning how far one wished to go in search of various kinds of game, how resources need to be shared by a group to go beyond 'varmit' hunting to a larger game, how differentiation of labor can come about in weapon-making and weapon-using, how one must decide among different odds in hunting in one terrain or another. Given the form of the game, its content can be readily varied to fit the conditions of life of other hunting groups, such as the Eskimo, again with the object of contrast.

> What has proved particularly interesting in our early work with the game is that it permits the grouping of a considerable amount of 'real' material around it—accounts of the life of the Kalahari Bushmen (of which there is an extraordinary rich record on film and in both literary and monographic form), their myths and art, the 'forbiddingly' desert ecology that is their environment.[1]

One fascinating exception to the rule (and surely notable because of its rarity as well as its quality) is the new primary program currently being developed by C. J. Margerison, a young English sociologist, and his primary-teacher wife.

[1] J. Bruner, *Man: A Course of Study*. Cambridge, Massachusetts: Educational Services, Inc., 1965, pp. 14–15.

Essentially, the Margerisons feel that young children *can* learn about society in a meaningful, interesting and intellectually appropriate form. Their 'syllabus' is built around the concept of society as an inter-related system. One learning experience or activity begins by having each seven-year-old in a given class 'make a man' out of pipe cleaners. The children give their men names and occupations. Eventually, they construct a house for each, and place the houses together to form a simple 'society'. At this point they attempt to discuss some of the problems involved in living in their 'society'—how will each man get what he needs to live? How will he pay for things? What will people use as payment? How will we keep people from simply taking what they want? etc. The Margerisons feel that they can thus deal with concepts such as division of labor and interdependence, among others. They are in the process of creating a series of similar activities designed to develop other basic social science understandings, and their work appears to be an excellent example of the sort of experimentation that seems to be generally lacking in primary school studies here.

A seventh criticism arises specifically out of my study of materials used in the more traditional teaching of geography although the point probably applies to other areas as well. It has to do essentially with the deterministic nature of geography and the resultant neglect of *man* and his role in affecting the 'character' of a given place. When other countries *are* studied, a great deal of attention is given to comparing certain places that have established sharply contrasting patterns of life, and that are located in vastly differing physical environments—for example, New York vs. the Australian outback. One seldom (if ever) sees comparisons made between places with contrasting physical settings inhabited by societies with strong cultural similarities (e.g., Lancaster, England and interior New South Wales, Australia, or San Diego, California and Boston, Massachusetts). Similarly, comparisons are seldom made between places having similar physical environments but occupied by people with substantially different cultures (e.g., Tucson, Arizona and Fes, Morocco).

This seems to be still another reflection of the lack of concern here for the contributions of the other social sciences—in this case, sociology and anthropology in particular. Without some attention to the anthropological point of view, and in particular to the concept of 'culture', children end up with a treatment of other people and places that is, essentially, descriptive—and invidious comparisons can, and often are, made between 'us and them'. A good deal of time and attention needs to be given to such studies if children are not to come away from them with the feeling that 'simple' societies are somehow less than human or inferior to their own.

A final concern is exemplified best, I think, by a description of an afternoon spent in what was in many ways a fascinating primary school in rural Leicestershire. During the entire afternoon the school's 'juniors' (the group I observed) were free to carry out projects that were of interest to them. There was a great deal of arts and crafts activity—carpentry, weaving, block printing, etc. The children were obviously well-behaved, busy, and interested in their work. Yet I couldn't help but feel that this happy, involved group of children were somehow existing in the middle of what we all know to be a terribly complex, rapidly changing world—completely divorced from its reality, protected from its problems, and uninvolved in its conflicts and dilemmas.

When organized social studies topics *are* explored in English primary schools, what might be called their 'conflict' content appears to be carefully 'censored'; one studies the 'nomads of the hot desert lands', and why they move from place to place—but one does *not* study the problems of mobility in our own changing society. One carefully charts 'traffic patterns' in a local study, but one does not discuss the *problems* caused by the mass production or the motor car or the ways in which it has changed our lives. One lists the services and amenities available in a given community, but one does *not* discuss their adequacy, quality, or the possible need for their improvement. One reads a sample study about a California farm which leaves out any mention of the problems faced by Mexican braceros, the possible effects of automation on agriculture in this area, or the changing life-ways of the farm family. One uses textbooks (and other books) that ignore the human diversity that exists now and continues to grow in England; textbooks that in Nicolas Hawke's words, are 'deplorably out of date and continue to propagate the racial and international attitudes of colonial days'.[1]

The real world, of course, exists, and no school, no teacher, no syllabus will ever completely isolate children from it. Yet the school's responsibility would seem to include some attempts at increasing children's awareness of the inadequacies and inequalities that exist in both their local and their wider environments. Failing this, children will, of course, muddle through, picking up ideas and attitudes wherever they find them and becoming more and more aware (perhaps through harsh personal experience) about the conflict that exists between the school world and the real world.

None of this suggests, incidentally, that American primary schools have been any more effective in bringing this kind of reality to the classroom than have their English counterparts. Nevertheless, the problem seems to me to be a real one in both countries, and an awareness that it exists is at least a necessary preliminary to positive action.

Finally, the relevant suggestions and observations contained in the two volume, twelve hundred page report of the Central Advisory Council for Education—the Plowden Report—must, of course, be considered in any analysis of this kind. Its recommendations represent the most recent thinking of large numbers of England's most influential and respected educators, and an examination of their views will surely be of help as one attempts to look into the immediate curricular future.

One might begin one's analysis by looking through the index and table of contents for references to 'Social Science', 'Anthropology', 'Sociology', 'Economics', and 'Political Science'. I did; and, despite the concern expressed (in the section on the 'Aims of Primary Education') for an education that would, among other things, help children cope with social and economic change, critically analyze their own society, understand the nature of a democratic society, etc.. etc.—I could find *no* reference to *any* of these disciplines. This straightforward omission states the committee's views far more eloquently, I think, than would an explanatory paragraph or two. Obviously, in Plowden's view, the insights of the social sciences are not

[1] N. Hawkes, *Immigrant Children in British Schools*. London: Pall Mall Press, 1966, p. 12.

perceived of as necessary, useful, or appropriate segments of the primary school curriculum.

I find it exceedingly difficult to imagine how one learns to either understand, predict, or cope with economic, social or political change without utilizing these disciplines. The anthropologists' creation and continuing refinement of the concept of culture for example, seems to me to be a profound contribution to man's intellectual arsenal—and an essential idea that must be grasped if one is to begin to understand the lifeways of other people. Yet the section devoted to geography in the body of the Report makes no mention of the ways in which geographers are utilizing concepts drawn from anthropology, economics, and the other social sciences.

The same criticism applies to Plowden's treatment of history. Most historians would agree for example, that the events that followed on the heels of the European discovery and settlement of the new world can be made much clearer if they are perceived of as examples of culture conflict. In other words, given an understanding of the total culture of a given group of American Indians—what they believed to be 'good' or 'bad', who and how they worshipped, the way they valued and utilized land, etc.—one cannot only understand the clashes between Indian and white man, but one might even *predict* what was likely to occur—and more importantly what might occur in another situation in which similar conditions existed.

To continue our critical analysis of the Plowden Report, we find expression in a number of places of the fear that seems to grip many English educationalists when even a broad pattern of learning experiences is outlined in advance—when the curriculum is 'structured' or blocked out to guarantee that topics of worth and significance are in fact dealt with and that overt and meaningless repetition will not take place. Interestingly enough, while the geography and history sections warn the reader that children '*do not* offer explanations' and '*will not* talk about cause and effect' (italics mine), the mathematics section inform us that 'children show a capacity for mathematical thinking and for processes formally regarded as advanced much earlier than was ever dreamed of . . . such things as number series, sets . . . and the geometry of shapes now appear in the primary school curriculum'.

Other statements that seem to contradict the premises upon which primary social studies are supposed to rest include these:

Problems are given . . . in raw form with the idea of learning a mathematical concept.

The old . . . problems were often concerned with irrelevant situations . . . (that) involved no constructive thinking, only the choice and application of a process.

(There is) the necessity for a very carefully thought out scheme of work in junior schools.

In mathematics, then, order, sequence, advanced thinking, concept development and a mathematical curriculum drawn from and based upon 'pure mathematics' or what might be called the mathematics of mathematicians seem to be the accepted order of things. History and geography are not conceived in this way, and there appears to be acceptance of the notion that these fields of study as taught to children in schools have little, if anything in common.

In summary, then the Plowden Report contains no mandate for radical change as far as history and geography are concerned. Although clichéd appeals for 'more world geography' and 'less rigid subject-matter division' appear again in Plowden, a truly agonizing reappraisal has not been called for at this time.

Because of space limitations I have neglected to treat private primary schools in general, or that uniquely English invention, the private preparatory school. This should not suggest that their place in the scheme of things is either unimportant or ineffectual. On the other hand, the vast majority of English children *do* attend maintained primary schools, and a reasonably adequate treatment of their approaches to social studies precludes a similar treatment of private schools. For the purposes of this chapter, we will have to satisfy ourselves with the generalization that considerable diversity exists; many private schools follow the developmental, child-centered patterns described above, while others (particularly the preparatory schools) are far more traditional, far more subject-centered.

Neither have I discussed the growing importance of the BBC radio and television programs for the schools, and the possibilities they offer for improving social studies education here. The activities of organizations such as the Parliamentary Group for World Government and the Conference of Christian and Jews have been ignored, as have other groups and individuals who are or who will be playing a role in improving social studies offerings in primary schools.[1]

Nevertheless, I have tried to deal with what appear to me to be overriding issues and concerns related to the study of man and society. In doing so I have, of course, ignored much that is good. This is, indeed, a pity, since (in my judgment) English primary education at its best is unparalleled anywhere. One can only hope that some of the questions raised here may bring about a reappraisal of existing practice that may, perhaps, make it even better.

[1] At this writing both the Schools Council and the Nuffield Foundation are supporting exploratory projects in primary social studies. Of particular interest is the new Schools Council project headed by Geoffrey Caston.

III: SOCIAL STUDIES IN SECONDARY SCHOOLS: HISTORY

WHILE SOME social scientists (as well as numbers of social studies sympathizers and other 'fellow travelers') have criticized the inherent inadequacies of history as virtually the sole means of acquainting English youngsters with 'man and society' it is precisely on these grounds that history's supporters defend her. That is, they see history as a truly integrating discipline that includes elements of all the social sciences and welds them into a meaningful, logical pattern. Presumably, it would be possible to organize a history syllabus that *did* far more adequately deal with the contributions of social science than do existing courses of study; on the other hand, such syllabuses are more spoken about than taught. Those few that do exist may well be an improvement over earlier, narrower patterns; whether or not they *do* in fact treat the social sciences in any adequate manner remains a debatable issue.

A considerable majority of secondary schools of *all* kinds follow traditional programs in history, emphasizing a chronological treatment of British history with a fairly liberal sprinkling of modern European history.[1] At one particularly good girls' school (St Paul's in London) for example, *all* the children take a five year sequence (ages eleven to fifteen) in British and European history, meeting twice a week for 35 minutes classes. Two fairly typical history patterns are presented below:

COURSE A	COURSE B
Year 1. English history to 1485.	The early civilizations (to the Roman Empire).
Year 2. The Tudors and Stuarts.	English history to 1485.
Year 3. The eighteenth century.	Tudors and Stuarts.

[1] See F. J. Dwyer, *The Teaching of History in Secondary Schools*. London: Routledge, Kegan and Paul for *The Historical Association*, 1964, p. 15.

Year 4. Nineteenth-century   (and   The eighteenth century.
possibly twentieth-century)
Britain.
Year 5. Nineteenth-century   (and   Nineteenth-century   (and
possibly twentieth-century)   possibly twentieth-century)
Europe.   Britain and/or Europe.[1]

If one were to look below the surface of the stark outlines presented above, one would find that, in general, the grammar and private schools tend to emphasize political history. Their actual courses of study (naturally enough) resemble the various A and O level G.C.E. syllabuses, and of course, reflect their curriculum patterns and biases. Children in non-selective schools are often given a good deal more *social* and sometimes economic history than are their grammar school counterparts, the assumption being, one must conclude, that political history is more challenging or rigorous, and therefore, more suited to the academically able.

Since the school leaving age in Britain remains at this writing at fifteen, and since even for those who remain in school beyond the compulsory age, history becomes an optional subject by about the age of fourteen or fifteen, it follows that a large proportion of secondary school pupils will have 'completed' their exposure to history in any formal sense at a relatively tender age. Whether chronologically organized, largely pre-1914, essentially *British* history (and, generally, geography) represents the most adequate preparation for assuming the burdens of citizenship in a modern democracy is, at the very least, a debatable proposition. Nevertheless, it remains the pattern here.

This is not to say that other approaches do not exist; they do. Many thoughtful and creative teachers are able to extend the boundaries of their seemingly binding traditional syllabuses to include relevant history as well as appropriate material from other, related disciplines. Sixth formers may well find themselves, for example, exploring at depth concepts such as 'revolution', 'justice', and 'equality'—concepts that transcend the bounds of any given discipline. Similarly, students at this level

---

[1] *The Teaching of History in Secondary Schools.* Issued by The Incorporated Association of Assistant Masters in Secondary Schools. Cambridge: Cambridge University Press, 1965, p. 15.

often come to grips with the perplexing problems of historiography, particularly as they may relate to the problems of the modern historian as he goes about the task of writing history.

Some schools are developing history syllabuses that are a good deal more world-minded and more 'recent' than their more traditional predecessors. This syllabus, developed at Haberdasher's Aske's School in Elstree, Middlesex, is perhaps, illustrative:

SECOND YEAR

The Renaissance to the Scientific Revolution

1st Term: 1. The decline of the Middle Ages and Feudalism.
           2. The Renaissance.
           3. The Reformation—Europe and England.

2nd Term: 4. The Age of Discoveries. It is suggested that this topic lends itself well to the project method. However it is taught, it is hoped that emphasis will be placed on the civilizations discovered as well as the discoveries themselves. Suggested topics: why people explored; ships, instruments and maps; lives of great explorers; the Far East; the Americas; Africa; extent of overseas empire of European countries by 1600 and the effect this had on all parts of the world.

3rd Term: 5. Wars of Religion.
           6. Development of nation states. Absolutism, e.g. France and Louis XIV.
           7. Breakthrough of scientific ideas.
           8. Colonial expansion of Europe to 1700.

THIRD YEAR

England 1603–c. 1815 and development of modern powers.

1st Term: 1. The seventeenth-century English revolution.
           2. Study of eighteenth-century England probably by patch method—see suggested plan.

2nd Term   Choice of TWO of the following courses, which
and   have been taught in the third year for some time.

3rd Term: 3. Russia, especially from Peter the Great to *c.* 1917.
           4. British Empire and Commonwealth. Special study of India would be valuable within this.

FOURTH YEAR

Nineteenth-century England and Europe; the twentieth century.

Careful selection of topics is obviously essential here. Personal preferences of staff will lead to different choices and what follows is by way of suggestion.

1st Term: England in the nineteenth century.
   1. Industrial and agricultural revolutions.
   2. Social, economic, and political problems arising from economic changes: *Laissez-faire*; free trade; factory reform; parliamentary reform; trades unionism; education Chartism; industrial development in nineteenth century. This would involve some teaching of great men of the time, who may be thought to be indispensible.
   3. Alternatively a project on either great figures of nineteenth century or Britain and the world in nineteenth century or social problems in nineteenth-century Britain, in which information was charted and essays given some point would be of benefit.

2nd Term: Europe in the nineteenth century.
   1. Causes and course of French Revolution.
   2. Napoleon.
   3. Metternich's Europe.
   4. Liberalism, nationalism and revolution of 1848.
   5. Unification of Italy and Germany.
   6. Growing tensions in Europe leading to First World War.

3rd Term: Europe and the World, 1914+
   1. First World War. Treaty of Versailles, etc.
   2. League of Nations.
   3. The Great Depression, 1929–33.
   4. The Rise of Hitler, fall of Weimar Republic and Hitler's Germany—1939.
   5. Outline of inter-war Britain.
   6. Causes of Second World War.

The 'patch' or, in American terms, 'post-hole' approach is gaining favor as well, as these excerpts from the Sutton High School syllabus illustrate:

Here, English history is taught on the patch system in an attempt to give a broader and more detailed knowledge of all the aspects of certain important epochs than can be given in the time allotted if a continuous outline of events is taught. This is a flexible system within which the interests of the pupils can be developed and project work carried out. Each patch takes a term, and a time chart of the intervening periods links one patch with another; in this way, and by constant comparison of the ideas of one age with those of another, a sense of continuity may be preserved, and an understanding of the gradual evolution of English society may be gained. Charts, pictures, and filmstrips are used to illustrate the lessons and there is co-operation with the Geography, English, and Art departments on every possible occasion. The periods at present taught are:

In Upper III: 1. The Norman Conquest, 1066–1100.
2. The Chaucerian Age, 1340–99.
3. The Renaissance Period, 1450–1588 (for social life either take late C15 or part of C16).

In Lower IV: 1. The Later Stuarts (for social life either the reign of Charles II or that of Queen Anne). When possible, the B.B.C. Work Unit on Charles II will be followed.
2. A course of elementary civics covering Central; and
3. Local Government, the Legal System, and the Commonwealth.

In Upper IV: The Georgian Era from about 1750.
1. Social life and industrial and agricultural revolutions.
2. The development of the Empire overseas, including the loss of the American colonies. When possible the B.B.C. Work Unit on the Empire in India will be followed.
3. The French Revolution and Napoleon, 1789–1815.

Having taken this initial look at the *general* situation in history in English secondary schools, it might be useful to interject at this point a few descriptions of specific classroom observations. Since in this case we are concerned with classroom practice *per se*, I have chosen those observations that made particular impressions upon me, regardless of the type, size, philosophy, or function of the schools in question.

SUTTON HIGH SCHOOL

Located near the center of a bustling, attractive suburban community in Surrey, this fairly large (900 students) independent girls' school impresses one immediately with its order, its well-kept buildings and grounds, its wholesome atmosphere, and its purposefulness. Everyone, from the headmistress to the students in lower forms seems busily involved in the normal, everyday activities of the school. As is often true in English girls' schools (maintained *or* independent) the staff and headmistress seem particularly devoted to their school and their girls. The school is to them more a total part of their lives than is the case with most American teachers.

There is no streaming at Sutton, although setting does take place in a number of subjects. The range of ability is reasonably wide, including girls of slightly above average ability as well as many with intelligence test scores in the highest range.

The history class I observed consisted of a group of thirteen- and fourteen-year-olds who had been studying early nineteenth century industrial and social life in England. While teacher centered 'chalk and talk' lessons were anything but uncommon, the teacher tried to keep this to a minimum and to encourage a more active, imaginative role on the part of her children. In this case they had just completed a project involving the creation of a series of fascinating 'newspapers' that might have been published in the London of 1800–1825. For example, one paper was dated Friday, February 10, 1815. It included exceedingly well written stories on Napoleon Bonaparte's escape, the trial of a wealthy industrialist who was accused of abusing children working for him, reviews of 'new' books, advertisements, theatre critics comments on 'new' plays, a special feature on Edmund Keane and his 'triumph' in Othello, etc. All in all, the group seemed happy, alert, and interested, and history was apparently regarded as a stimulating school subject.

DARTINGTON SCHOOL

Dartington is now and has been a leader in educational innovation here. To begin with it is (along with Bedales and perhaps a few others) a rare phenomenon in England—a co-educational boarding school. Educationally, the staff is devoted to the fullest development of each individual, and it might be said the school is child-centered in the very best sense of that often mis-used term. There are no uniforms, and dress is disconcertingly casual. Students are responsible not only for doing a reasonable share of cleaning and maintenance duties, but also share in real decision-making situations concerned with the regulation of student conduct. The school has a particularly strong program in music, art and drama and evidence of this strength is to be seen (and heard!) everywhere.

It was at Dartington that I observed a man who must certainly be among the most stimulating teachers that I (or anyone else) has ever watched at work. The particular class I visited was a group of fourteen-year-olds who were studying the war of 1812. As he introduced the class to the topic, he used a number of large, cleverly drawn 'cartoons' of his own creation to illustrate various points. He quickly made 'connections' between the problem of neutral rights in 1812 and in World War I and moved freely into economics, sociology, and geography whenever this seemed appropriate. He consistently forced his students to defend statements they had made (or written), and even exposed his class to a number of fascinating first-hand accounts of *American* impressions of the war.

In discussing his conception of history, he emphasized the importance of dealing with a few 'big' ideas rather than teaching 'outline' history. He wanted more non-British accounts of history; accounts in which England, too, appears as the 'dirty dog'; he is concerned that children learn to think and read critically and that they learn to use reference works with precision. He feels that the other social sciences make history come alive, and that concentrating on political history alone emasculates the discipline. His office is a veritable treasure house of well organized teaching materials of all kinds that he and his students use—for example, cartoons, portraits, maps, time lines, contemporary (and his own, original) poems, 'test-yourself booklets', songs of the Irish Rebellion, French Revolution, California Gold Rush, etc., home made 'reference books' on literally dozens of topics, such as the one on the 'American Revolution' which consisted of clippings of maps, brief articles, contemporary paintings, etc.

This was perhaps one of the rare occasions in my experience in education (both in England and in the U.S.) where children seemed genuinely to enjoy the study of history, to be sorry when class had ended, and to look forward eagerly to tomorrow's class.

SEVENOAKS SCHOOL

At once both a 'public' and a maintained grammar school, Sevenoaks lies midway between the state and the private sector of education. Half of its 600 boys are eleven plus successes who enter the school at the age of eleven from the maintained area primary schools. The other half enter at thirteen as 'private' students, having been selected on the basis of the common entrance examination.

Sevenoaks is not a particularly impressive school in a purely physical sense. Its buildings are scattered about a busy road leading to nearby London, and they lack the charm of those at schools like Dartington. It is nevertheless, an intellectually stimulating, innovative, exciting place to be in. Its headmaster has gathered together an active, restive faculty who seem to revel in the school's role as a challenger of the existing order. The new mathematics program, the 'technical activities' center and the international house (among other developments) testify to the continued activity of headmaster and staff.

In this instance I visited a sixth form which was in the midst of a study of the American Revolution. The class consisted of about 18 boys who had been using a collection of primary source materials dealing with a number of related historical 'problems' as the basis for their essays which were to be handed in at this time. The atmosphere in the class was relaxed and informal. The history master explored certain aspects of the revolution through a meaty, knowledgeable, sophisticated lecture of about 20 minutes duration. During the course of the lecture, he explained that some of the difficulties between England and America were merely problems of communication, i.e., it was physically difficult to conduct a political dialogue across the Atlantic Ocean at that time. This point was immediately challenged by one boy as an inadequate explanation, since, after all, this was true of communication *everywhere* in the late eighteenth century, and therefore it clarified the problem very little indeed. The teacher took time to discuss the criticism and then allowed the class to discuss (for my benefit as a visitor) their reaction to sixth form history and the way it was taught at Sevenoaks. The boys immediately launched into a sophisticated, uninhibited, and critical discussion of the ways in which the master's biases had crept into his teaching, citing a number of specific examples that they had, apparently, recorded in their notes. There was never, during this discussion, any hint of disrespect for the teacher either as an historian or as an individual. On the contrary, one had the feeling that he was delighted with their performance and that they had indeed begun to learn something of the nature of history as he conceived it.

These experiences were, to this observer, at least, exceedingly positive. Of course, there were occasions where the very opposite of what I described took place. Nevertheless, the sort of teaching (and learning) that I have written about does illustrate some of the strengths of English education, and I would like to explore this positive side more fully.

While a good deal of criticism has been levelled both here and abroad at what might be termed nationalistic, 'Anglocentric' history,[1] there is considerable evidence that English education may well be less overtly nationalistic than that of other modern nations. On a purely subjective level, one cannot help but be impressed with the apparent tolerance of divergent political views that exists here. For example, the Communist Party, as weak and ineffectual as it is, continues to hold political meetings and enter candidates in local and national elections. These are duly reported in English newspapers, which give such events about as much space as they deserve—neither

[1] See, for example, R. A. Billington, *Anglo-American Misunderstanding, The Historian's Contribution To*. New York: Hobbs, Dorman and Company, 1966.

exaggerating their 'threat' nor ignoring their existence. At Sevenoaks International House, a bonafide young Hungarian Communist is a fully accepted member of the student body— something that would most certainly be unique in American educational experience.

A recent study carried out at the University of London provides more objective evidence. In essence, this was an investigation of nationalism in secondary education in England and Iraq. A randomly selected sample of about 1,000 English secondary school students and teachers (as well as a small number of university students) were asked to agree or disagree with a series of statements like these:

> School children should be educated to love and respect the peoples of all nationalities.

> Cultural interchange among nations are fruitful.
> True patriotism and internationalism are not incompatible.[1]

In addition, the subjects completed a series of open-ended statements dealing with similar questions.

Following a thorough analysis of the data, Hillmi concluded that:

> . . . Englishmen regard patriotism as a matter of course . . . they have hardly deemed it necessary, let alone educationally sound, for their schools to function as nurseries for patriots . . . the English seem to think that any deliberate and conscious inculcation into the minds of their children of certain nationalistic beliefs would ultimately amount to political indoctrination . . . [English schools do not] force the child . . . to believe in a particular formula for democracy, or to make him politically obliged to any national or international organization. It is not the school's function to propagate any ideological doctrine, whether democratic or otherwise. [Instead, they attempt to cultivate in their students] a sense of responsibility and loyalty, both toward his national ideals and institutions *and* to those of humanity in general. He is trained to appreciate other's opinions and to be tolerant toward points of view different from his own.[2]

---

[1] H. S. Hillmi, *Nationalism and Secondary Education in England and Iraq.* Unpublished Ph.D. Thesis, University of London Institute of Education, 1965, p. 421.
[2] Ibid., pp. 156, 165.

The implications for American education must, of course, be obvious.

Another strength that has already been hinted at in this chapter is the quality of work carried out in many English sixth forms. Small classes, a highly selected student body representing only a tiny proportion of the age-group, well-educated teachers with a mature concept of the nature of history—all combine to bring about a kind of education that is, at its best, unparalleled.

Those studying history in the sixth form at A level are expected to concentrate on a limited number of historical periods in considerable depth, and the following syllabus is, perhaps, illustrative of the scope of A level history as taught in British sixth forms:

Advanced Level
There will be three papers of 3 hours each.
Paper I. English History.
Either Paper IA. One of the following periods of English History:

(1)	450–1270	(5)	1714–1832
(2)	1270–1529	(6)	1815–1922
(3)	1529–1642	(7)	1865–1955
(4)	1643–1714		

Or Paper IB. One of the following outline periods of English History:

(8)	1529–1815	(9)	1714–1955

Paper II. European History.
Either Paper IIA. One of the following periods of European History.

(1)	395–1216	(5)	1715–1830
(2)	1216–1516	(6)	1815–1923
(3)	1516–1661	(7)	1871–1954
(4)	1610–1725		

Or Paper IIB. One of the following outline periods of European History:

(8)	1516–1789	(9)	1715–1954

In all papers each section will contain twelve questions and candidates must answer five questions from any one section.
The limiting dates of the periods must not be taken too rigidly. Candidates will be expected to have some knowledge of the years before and after the period chosen.

Paper II. Special Subject.

Special knowledge will be required of one of the following subjects. Candidates must answer four questions on the subject chosen: a choice of questions will be given. The special subjects are revised from time to time; for Summer, 1967, and January, 1968, they will be:

(1) Roman Britain.
(2) Twelfth-century monasticism in the West.
(3) The Age of Discovery, 1400–1550.
(4) The Renaissance in Britain in the sixteenth century.
(5) France in the age of Richelieu and Mazarin.
(6) Scientific and technological development in Britain, 1660–1760.

> The main achievements of British scientists and technologists, with special references to their application to industries (e.g. agriculture, metallurgy, textiles, transport and communications) and the economic and social results. Candidates will be expected to have some knowledge of developments in Europe in the same period.

(7) English social conditions in the second half of the eighteenth century.
(8) The causes and course of the French Revolution, 1774–99.
(9) The history of the United States of America, 1783–1865.
(10) The history of the British Empire during the reign of Queen Victoria.
(11) English social conditions in the second half of the nineteenth century.
(12) The making of the Triple Alliance and the Triple Entente.[1]

This tells us very little, however, about the ultimate goals of history teaching in the sixth form. Essentially, this course of study is intended to serve as the basis for further study at the university level. These syllabuses are *not* geared to 'citizenship training', and one does *not* assume that a student's education may cease after a year or two in the sixth form (although in fact, it often does). Students doing A level history must be

[1] Regulations and Syllabuses for the General Certificate of Education Examinations, Summer, 1967 and January 1968. University of London.

viewed as potential historians, and their program of study is designed to encourage independence of thought, facility with a great variety of historical materials, and the ability to make reasoned assessments of such material. Obviously, this is an ideal that is never achieved (or even approached) in some sixth forms. Others, however, come close indeed, and observing such classes in action is surely one of the most exciting educational experiences available to visitors from abroad.

Other strengths might well be noted—for example, some of the beautiful publications of the Historical Association, or the creative and imaginative programs developed by the BBC, the well-equipped 'history rooms' one often sees, as well as the intelligent way in which England's wealth of local resources are utilized in historical studies. Perhaps, however, it would more helpful to turn at this point to criticism rather than additional praise.

At the end-of-term prize-giving festivities at a Yorkshire secondary school I heard a professor from a neighbouring college deliver the 'inspirational', main-event speech that was to send all the students home with a new zest for learning. The speaker gave considerable emphasis to the importance of *memorizing*. 'Nothing was more essential to academic success', he said, and he launched into a detailed, nostalgic recollection of how he had learned to memorize more effectively when he was a boy. It seemed as if someone had purposely attempted to epitomize the stereotypes that many Americans hold concerning English education—and surely the speaker could not have caricatured English education any more effectively if he had consciously tried to do so.

I hope I have seen enough of classroom procedures here to put this particular speech in proper perspective. Nevertheless, it does illustrate a problem that neither English nor American teachers have been able to solve to everyone's satisfaction. Certainly even the most cursory evaluation of O and A level G.C.E. examination papers indicates an unusual emphasis on one's ability to recall a given 'right' answer. Neither do the newer C.S.E. examinations appear to be a great deal better in this respect.

It seemed to me that in far too many classrooms there was a preoccupation with questions like 'What was Pitt the Elder's attitude toward Europe?' 'What was his attitude toward Walpole?' and 'How did he fall from power?' In most cases, responding to such questions did *not* involve sifting through a number of opinions, discussing or evaluating them, or possibly suggesting alternative hypotheses. There was one 'right' answer to each question, and it probably follows in the student's view that there must be one right answer to most historical questions. This approach leads inevitably to a form of fact-cramming that is, at best, dull and discouraging to many students. At its worst it becomes a grossly anti-intellectual exercise that mitigates against any real understanding of history.

To some extent, this criticism must be related to the rather inflexible, Piaget dominated, 'developmental stages' concept of children's intellectual powers that was discussed more fully in the preceding section on primary education. The more complex thinking processes or strategies, i.e., evaluating, categorizing, generalizing, hypothesizing—all of these are seen to be essentially beyond the intellectual range of most students below the sixth form. This attitude persists despite considerable evidence to the contrary,[1] and we find that many English educators persist in viewing the sixth form as the real turning point—the place where 'pupils' become 'students' and, perhaps, instruction becomes education.

The evidence indicating that the development of more complex thinking skills is a *continuous* task that is greatly facilitated by a sequential educational program is powerful indeed.[2] Nevertheless, in my judgment, far too little attention is being paid here to the development of planned educational experiences designed to gradually yet *continuously* extend children's thinking abilities.

Similar assumptions are often made about secondary school children's interests; consider, for example, this statement in a

[1] See chapter on primary education.

[2] See, for example, W. Gardner and V. Rogers 'Learning Principles', a working paper developed for *Project Social Studies*, The University of Minnesota, Minneapolis, Minnesota. This paper explores at some length the implications of current research related to the development of thought processes in children. For a still more inclusive analysis, the appropriate sections of D. Russell's *Children's Thinking*. New York: Ginn and Company, 1956 should be explored.

recent publication of the Department of Education and Science:[1]

> In their *later* teens . . . (secondary school children) are *beginning* to be interested in social and political problems . . . [italics mine].

My experiences here indicate that this is simply *not* true, and the planning of curricular experiences in history on the *assumption* that thirteen, fourteen and fifteen-year-old children are *not* interested in relevant, perhaps more recent, social economic, political and other problems is simply indefensible.

Another point that surely needs further exploration is implied in Ian Lister's sardonic comments in *Crisis in the Humanities*:

> To date, the basic idea behind many history courses in the schools was that pupils should grow up with history: small boys lived in the Roman era, feudalism and short trousers were left at about the same stage, and those lucky ones who lasted in the course [and] who were not made neurotic by gaps in their [past] were smiling and integrated as they broke into Modern Times when they left school on their way to the Labour Exchange.[2]

In essence, more recent history—particularly the period from the end of World War II to the present—has tended to be neglected, despite a strong and steady undercurrent of criticism of such practices. There is a tendency to avoid 'leaving anything out', to be inclusive rather than selective in syllabus construction, and to make assumptions about the length of time most pupils will in fact study history which are simply not borne out by experience. Since large numbers of English children in *all* kinds of schools drop history by the age of fourteen, more attention might be given to the creation of more selective, required courses that will *guarantee* some reasonable amount of attention to more recent history by the end of the fourth year of secondary school. Failing this, and with the raising of the school leaving age, history might become a required, all-the-way through subject, thus allowing six years

[1] *Citizens Growing Up*. London: Her Majesty's Stationery Office, 1949, p. 77.

[2] J. H. Plumb, Editor, *Crisis in the Humanities*. London: Penguin Books, 1964, p. 159.

of study—which surely ought to permit adequate attention to the modern period. Other solutions (and those least likely to find favor with English historians) include the development of broader 'social studies' courses that may treat the contemporary world more generously.

In any event, the fact remains that history is, for many English secondary school students, the only *systematic* exposure they will have to the economic, social, and political problems involved in human existence—past or present. The geographers often strive valiantly to broaden the coverage of their discipline but geography cannot be an adequate substitute for the types of questions and problems that seem to fall so much more naturally into history's domain. Given this situation, and given the fact that *all* English children will grow up eventually to become participating members of a democratic society, it seems that a great deal of attention needs to be focused on the question, 'What kind of history for the *non-historian*?'

Perhaps related to everything that has already been said is the question of the very nature of history itself as it is conceived by English educators. W. H. Burston perhaps expresses the dominant view in these words:

> Unlike mathematics and science, each year's work in history is not in any important degree, raised upon the previous year's work, requiring constant reference back to it. History is not . . . a structural subject. It is rather a subject where more advanced study consists of more mature, and more profound, interpretation of any period of history.[1]

One might compare the implication of Burston's statement with this brief excerpt from a descriptive paper outlining the content for one unit or 'topic' of an American *history* course for twelve-year-old children:

> *Unit One: Indian America*
> Pre-white contact Indian cultures should be selected to demonstrate not only different life-ways involving different political, social, religious, and other patterns (at different levels of technological advancement) but also to provide significant bases for culture conflict as it developed between these cultures and the

---

[1] W. H. Burston, *Sixth Form History Teaching*. Routledge and Kegan Paul. Published for the Historical Association, 1963, p. 5.

Spanish, French, and English settlers in a later period. For these purposes, it was felt that three cultures involved the minimum possible number to both indicate diversity of pattern and yet provide the various basic combinations of early and late contact conditions for white European contact. The Aztec society illustrates a highly developed North American culture and is useful for early Spanish contact; the Iroquois show a semi-sedentary Indian tribe and early French and English contact; while the Plains Indians demonstrate horse culture on the plains and later Spanish and Anglo-American conflict. In each case the teacher is to develop the complete culture of the Indians as well as to compare the cultures in order to reinforce the culture-as-a-system idea. In addition, the teacher must stress the Indian way of life as a prelude to possible Indian-White conflict, accommodation, and acculturation.

The following pages do not treat each Indian culture in its entirety but rather outline those central themes of each society's culture that seem particularly teachable and will satisfy the criteria of both uniqueness and later Indian-White relations. In keeping with the entire course, building types, village layouts, and artifacts are used to engender interest in that society and to point to the larger patterns of that culture.[1]

It seems to me that if one has any intention at all of teaching history in a broader sense, i.e., attempting to teach about people and their past through the utilization of the insights of disciplines such as anthropology, sociology, economics, or psychology, one must begin somewhere to consider the ways in which such disciplines can contribute to a better understanding of history and, further, to isolate those concepts and generalizations that may be most useful to the student of history. Even a cursory look at Professor Berkhofer's brief statement reveals a concern for concepts such as conflict, accommodation, acculturation, and culture. In other units, other, similar concepts are used. If history itself is not a structured subject, surely the ideas or concepts that enable one to understand history need to be incorporated into courses of study in some systematic way. One *might* justify considerable study, for example, of the culture concept (through, perhaps,

[1] R. Berkhofer, *The Sixth Grade Curriculum*. Working paper developed for *Project Social Studies*. University of Minnesota, Minneapolis, Minnesota, 1965.

a study of the life-ways of a variety of families) before the formal study of history itself. One would surely find it difficult adequately to understand the relationship between the Indians and the White settlers in America without a thorough grasp of the idea of 'culture' as the anthropologist has developed it. None of this suggests that significant concepts such as these might not be developed simultaneously as a course in history evolved, or that history itself could not be a reasonable curricular vehicle to explore such ideas. It does seem, however, that there is a great need here for a serious search of history *and* the social sciences for significant ideas, concepts, generalizations, and work-ways of these disciplines. Having made such analyses, the selection of content, the broad 'ordering' of a course of study might well take on a more sequential, logical look, and teachers might find it easier to justify the topics they select for study and the emphases they give them.

One might add other criticisms—for example, many secondary modern school history programs consist either of watered-down versions of grammar school courses of study, or of excessively child-like studies of topics such as food, clothing, and housing 'through the ages' that lead in no particular direction, have no particular relevance to modern problems, cannot be justified by what we know about the interests of secondary school children, and surely develop few if any of the 'large central ideas' or concepts referred to above.

One finds, too, that 'local history' is considered sacred in many secondary schools (as it is in primary schools). This is not to suggest that the locality cannot or should not be exploited in the study of history. But again, there *is* more to the world than that which immediately surrounds us, and modern children have been introduced to the wider world through any number of media that did not exist 50 to 100 years ago. This is, of course, a matter of priorities, a matter of selection— perhaps a matter of more careful consideration of expected educational outcomes and more sequential courses of study. In any event, an undue devotion to local history can often lead to indefensible repetition at various age levels as well as boredom to those whose horizons have already broadened and who long to consider more significant studies related to the world beyond the town.

IV: SOCIAL STUDIES IN SECONDARY SCHOOLS: GEOGRAPHY

GEOGRAPHY HAS earned a place in the English academic sun that it has never managed to achieve in the United States. It stands as one of the more popular G.C.E. choices at both O and A levels, and it is a part of the curriculum of virtually all secondary schools, maintained and independent, selective and non-selective.

Ideally, geography as taught in the secondary modern school ought *not* to be a pale imitation of the grammar school course. Rather it is expected that those responsible for curricular development in such schools will develop programs suitable for the abilities and interests of their particular children. In general, one *does* observe the inclusion in the non-selective syllabus of a number of more limited topics for study that do, perhaps, enable the student to deal more with the 'concrete', e.g., studies of food supplies, houses, local industry, etc. Most non-selective schools, however, still give considerable attention to studies of the British Isles and Europe, while the courses of study for secondary modern school students who are working toward the G.C.E. would be similar, of course, to G.C.E. syllabuses in selective schools.

While most independent schools tend to deal with geography in essentially the same manner as do the maintained grammar schools, some see it as a subject not entirely worthy of equal status with history, English, Latin, or French. At the renowned and highly respected Winchester, for example, geography is considered more suitable for 'duller boys' and the G.C.E. examination is not offered in geography at either O or A level.

The following syllabuses (which ought not to be construed as representative) are at least examples of pre-sixth form programs in geography carried out in two secondary schools—the first a highly selective independent school, the second a secondary modern school.

ST PAUL'S GIRLS' SCHOOL GEOGRAPHY SYLLABUS—1965–66

Middle IV

1ST TERM

A study of sample regions of the British Isles. It is hoped during this term to lay the foundation for future study by acquiring a *basic geographical vocabulary and skills*, and providing a sound outline knowledge of the home region so that valid comparisons may be made with other areas of the world.

2ND TERM

Australia.

3RD TERM

South America.

During all three terms the work will include easy map reading and elementary physical geography, linked in each case to the regional studies and illustrating them.

Upper IV

1ST TERM

Africa.

2ND AND 3RD TERMS

Asia, with particular reference to the Middle East and Monsoon lands. Further map reading, using large-scale O.S. maps, and physical geography related to the regional studies.

Lower V

Map work using 1″ and 2½″ ordnance survey maps. Weather observation, and the synoptic charts of the daily weather report in relation to the climate of N.W. Europe and the British Isles.

Regional Geography of Europe, and associated physical geography, especially glacial erosion, river work, volcanoes, mountain building.

V

Regional Geography of the British Isles, including elementary geology and the effect of rocks on scenery.

Map Interpretation using 1″ and 1½″ ordnance survey maps, chosen to illustrate the regional studies. Field work, usually in the Box Hill area.

ISLINGTON GREEN SECONDARY SCHOOL

First Year

1. LOCAL STUDY

   (a) Map of area around the school introducing scales (pacing classrooms, accurate measuring), orientation and conventional signs.

   (b) Locating retail foodshops and mapping them. Each child to select a shop in the area and to investigate from where food items come. To note distribution from grower or manufacturer to wholesaler; from wholesaler to retailer; from retailer to consumer.

   (c) Keeping a pictorial record of such items in a scrapbook and encouraging written description of them to include country of origin, climate, and production.

2. USE OF ATLAS

   Latitude and longitude—place finding.

   The use of the atlas to locate places referred to in current affairs.

   The continent and oceans. Countries and their capitals.

3. THE BRITISH ISLES

   (a) Its size and position.

   (b) Climate.

   (c) Relief.

   (d) Some principal industries and compare where possible with local industries.

   Engineering (national and local).

   Clothing (national and local).

   Furniture making (national and local).

   (e) The Counties.

4. A CONTINENT: AUSTRALIA

   (a) Its size.

   (b) Regions and natural vegetation.

   (c) Climate.

   (d) Countries and islands within the continent.

   (e) Its people and occupations.

   (f) Natural resources.

   (g) Industries and development.

S.S.E.E.—6

5. A COMMONWEALTH COUNTRY: NEW ZEALAND
  (*a*) Its size and position. Distance from Britain. Voyage by sea; journey by air.
  (*b*) Tasman, Cook and the Maoris.
  (*c*) Relief two main islands, mountains, hills, plains, inlets.
  (*d*) Climate compared with Great Britain.
  (*e*) Vegetation and animals.
  (*f*) Farming.
  (*g*) Industries and mineral wealth.
  (*h*) Population.

6. ITEMS OF TOPICAL INTEREST
  E.g., a royal journey—map or route, countries visited. Meeting places of Statesmen, air travel and air ports.

Second Year

1. LOCAL STUDY
  Islington's industries. Children to supply details of factories known to them in Islington.

2. MAP READING
  Conventional signs.
  Scales.

3. USE OF ATLAS
  Points of compass; climate graphs; use of index; latitude and longitude.

4. EUROPE
  Position temperate latitudes.
  Habitable land.
  Access to sea.
  Mineral wealth.
  Its people.
  Countries and capitals.

5. ITALY
  Position.
  Natural divisions.
  Climate.
  Northern plain.
  Apennines.
  Southern Italy.
  Italian Islands.
  People of Italy and their occupations.
  Trade.

6. BRAZIL
>   Position.
>   Regions.
>   Coffee.
>   Mining.
>   Manufacturing industries.
>   Foreign trade.

7. ITEMS OF TOPICAL INTEREST
>   World populations and the need for greater food production.

Third Year

1. LOCAL STUDY
>   The boroughs of London—size and distribution of population.
>   Principal industries.

2. MAP READING
>   Conventional signs.
>   Scales, contours, enlarging a map.

3. USE OF ATLAS
>   Graphs—temperature and rainfall.
>   Use of Index, countries and their chief towns.

4. ASIA
>   Position and vastness.
>   Relief.
>   Climate.
>   Natural regions.
>   Countries and capitals.
>   Its people.
>   Occupations and industries.
>   Trading opportunities between East and West.

5. CHINA
>   Its growing importance due to its position, size and environment, population.
>   Trade between the United Kingdom and China.
>   Means of transport.
>   The importance of Hong Kong.

6. CANADA
>   To be treated as a project. Class to get own material—maps, statistics, etc.

7. ITEMS OF TOPICAL INTEREST
   Scrap-book for maps, cuttings, articles on general interest.

Fourth Year

1. LOCAL STUDY
   Islington—area, its neighboring boroughs, industries, wards, and parliamentary representation.
   London's boroughs—principal industries.
   London's wholesale markets.
   London's docks.

2. BRITISH ISLES
   Position and size.
   Physical features.
   Climate.
   Chief industries (including agriculture and fishing).
   Chief source of raw materials.
   Chief market and trade routes.

3. REGIONS OF THE WORLD
   World map—continents and oceans.
   Natural regions.
   Physical features.
   Climate and human conditions.
   Occupations of man in relation to those conditions.

4. MAPS
   The use of ordnance maps—reference points, scales contours, conventional signs.
   The atlas with its graphs and index.

5. NORTH-WEST EUROPE (the countries of France, Belgium, Luxembourg, The Netherlands, Germany, Switzerland, Denmark and Sweden).

6. ITEMS OF TOPICAL INTEREST

Again, it would seem useful to move at this point from general discussions of syllabuses and courses of study to descriptions of classroom practice. The two lessons described below occurred in schools with contrasting physical settings and vastly differing conceptions of their educational functions or purposes—nevertheless, I found each, in its own way, particularly rewarding:

GUILDFORD ROYAL GRAMMAR SCHOOL

The Guildford Royal Grammar School is divided into two parts by the High Street of one of Surrey's busiest trading and marketing centres. On one side of this bustling main street is the new building made of brick and designed in that rather nondescript 'modern' that seems so typical of many newer English secondary schools. On the other side of the High Street is a white sixteenth-century building that still houses usable classrooms and an almost priceless collection of ancient books, kept constantly under lock and key in its 'chained library'. Both buildings house about 500 boys who attend the school as day students, having been selected for grammar school places on the results of Surrey's eleven-plus examination.

While there is no streaming at Guildford, there is setting in most courses, and many of the more able boys take O levels at the end of the fourth form, skip the fifth, and therefore are enabled to spend three years in the sixth. Guildford also has a 'general' sixth for boys who will not be going to university, but who, nevertheless, want to accumulate a reasonable number of O level passes.

As with most English secondary schools, Guildford has a thoroughly equipped geography room, stocked with maps of all kinds, books, and periodicals. The geography department also runs its own, quite complete, weather station.

I observed a group of second formers (twelve-year-olds) who were in the midst of a study of Australia. The boys were divided into seven or eight small working groups, each of which had taken the responsibility for a given aspect of Australian geography. One group was in the process of illustrating and explaining climatic patterns, and a number of carefully drawn maps had been constructed to help explain wind currents, rainfall patterns, etc. Other groups charted the location of cities in relation to rainfall, proximity to the sea and other (largely physical) factors. Throughout the thirty-five or forty minute class the boys were free to chat quietly among themselves as they worked in their groups, and to move about the room as necessary. Their teacher moved from group to group, acting largely as a 'critical consultant', and the class as a whole seemed actively engaged in their study.

EASTFIELD SECONDARY SCHOOL

Eastfield is a secondary modern school, although that is not made clear in its official title. It is located in one of the older, poorer industrial sections of Wolverhampton. Since new school construction is expected in this area sometime in the not-too-distant (but as yet still rather indefinite) future, Eastfield must continue to utilize its present building and grounds. The building is located in the midst of slum housing that must be of at least Victorian vintage, along with a sprinkling of newer, local Government constructed council houses. There are virtually no playing fields here, and the children must take a twenty-minute bus ride to get to a location suitable for soccer or field hockey. The school building itself is as old as the slum housing that surrounds it. On the day I visited Eastfield, the *indoor* temperature was just over 40° F. in most rooms. Many children wore mittens in class, and in a science laboratory *all* of the burners glowed steadily and continuously—for heat rather than for science.

The staff (whom I met in an equally inadequate teacher's room) were a cheerful, energetic group who took all of this in stride, looked at their situation with a sense of humor, and for the most part, seemed deeply concerned about the education of Eastfield's children.

Streaming is the accepted pattern here, and the children are divided by ability into roughly five or six groups. However, since many of the area's academically clever children have been 'creamed off' and sent to selective schools, even Eastfield's A stream is not a particularly academic group, and the school offers *no* G.C.E. courses at any level.

While I was impressed with the staff as a whole, I was particularly moved by the teaching of a young geographer who had been brought up in this area and who seemed to feel a personal responsibility for the education of these children. He would be, in my judgment, an outstanding teacher in *any* school, for I saw him work with children of varying abilities at Eastfield. He was most effective, however, with a group of 'No. 3 C' children, over half of whom were virtually non-readers. He treated this class with the same dignity that some teachers reserve for 'high flyers' only, and they responded in kind. He explained, with infinite patience and care, how water gets into a well (part of a study of man's way of coping with his physical environment), slowly and deliberately sketching a diagram on the blackboard. One boy—a good looking, bright-eyed youngster of thirteen—showed us his notebook. He had dutifully copied as much as he could of his teacher's diagram and notes—but he could barely read any of it. Apparently a good deal of 'geography time' must be used by the teacher as an opportunity for further work in basic language skills, and he managed to devise a number of creative, interesting ways of doing so.

The class was at all times attentive and polite. During the last ten minutes they were allowed to talk to their visitor from America, and they plied me with questions about anything and everything American. At no time did the teacher suggest that these children were hopeless, or that they needed metal work or cooking rather than geography; on the contrary, he made every effort to bring some of the insights of geography to bear on their lives, and he was providing even this most difficult group with some of the elements of a liberal education.

The preceding descriptions are obviously only isolated examples of what were, to me, impressive though differing illustrations of classroom experience.

In a more general sense, I found the thoroughly organized, imaginatively planned field studies that are a part of many geography programs in English secondary schools among the most effective teaching procedures I have observed anywhere.

Some schools maintain their own field studies centers, but many take advantage of the superb facilities offered by the Field Studies Council.[1]

This non-profit organization has seven residential centers located in particularly scenic, unspoiled country that lend themselves admirably to the study of geography. The centers have laboratories, reference libraries, and equipment suitable for use in the field, as well as resident staffs of experienced teachers with a thorough knowledge of the area.

Forest Hill School, a large London boy's comprehensive, conducts geographical field courses for its students each year.

[1] Field Studies Council, 9 Devereux Court, Strand, London, W.C.2.

Their excursion to Walmer, Kent, lasted about ten days and included about thirty thirteen-year-old boys. An outline of their program is reproduced below:

GEOGRAPHICAL FIELDWORK GROUP, WALMER, KENT

Day	*Morning*	*Afternoon*	*Evening*
Tuesday		Assemble at Forest Hill School. Leave by coach for Walmer.	Unpack.
Wednesday	The local area. Inland and coastal mapping quiz.	Visit to Deal Castle. Free time in the town.	Recreation.
Thursday	Coach to Sandwich. Walk to Richborough.	Reculver—and Birchington Bay. Work on coastal erosion and defense.	Recreation and Reports.
Friday	Chalk country. Visit to Folkestone Warren. Downs behind Folkestone.	Fruit and hop farm study. Heart's Delight Farm. Kingston.	Games and Reports.
Saturday	Stour Valley. Parish Survey of Chilham. Transect. Land use. Building.	Survey of village. Free time in Canterbury.	Recreation.
Sunday	Church service in Walmer.	Recreation. Afternoon walk.	Preparation.
Monday	Romney Marsh. Sheep farm survey. Vinal Farm near Brenzett.	Rye. A town study.	Games and Reports.

Day	Morning	Afternoon	Evening
Tuesday	A day in Dover. Castle visit. Group work in the town.	Harbour study. Car Ferry Terminal.	Recreation and Reports.
Wednesday	Romney Marsh. Sketching point from old coastline. Lydd Airport (Silver City).	Coach and rail to Dungeness and lighthouse.	Recreation and Reports.
Thursday	Study and class-rooms period at hotel.	Visit to Goodwin Sands, or Ramsgate.	Recreation.
Friday	Free time in Deal.	Leave approx. 2 p.m. for London.	

Some idea of the sort of activities engaged in by students may be obtained from the following 'study guides':

COASTAL AND MAPPING QUIZ

Walk down Walmer Castle Road. Turn left at the bottom and take the first footpath on the right. As you walk along this footpath you will see parkland on your right. This is where your quiz begins.

1. What is building A? ....
2. What do you notice about the height of the road and the beach? ....
....
3. How many storm ridges can you observe near B? ....
4. (a) How many castle cannon guns are there on the first level above the road? ....
   (b) If the castle was once right on the sea-shore how does it come to be so far from the sea now? ....
5. Draw a section of the cliff at C. How deep is the soil? What is the base rock? ....
6. What type of house at D? ....
7. Name the road at E? ....
8. What are the building materials of the house at F? ....
....
9. Go down road G and mark on your map the position of the lifeboat station.
10. Fill in the correct sign for the church at H.

11. Fill in the correct sign at I.
12. What is the feature at J? Can you see any surface drainage?
....

13. What sort of slope would you describe K as being?...................
....

14. What is the feature of land-use at L?..................................
15. What is the number of the main road met beyond M?..............
....

   Where does it lead to? ....
16. What is the building at N? ....
17. Put in the sign for the church at O. What is it built of?...........
....

18. What is the building at P?..
19. What type of way is at Q?..
20. What type of way is at R?..

On Your Return
(*a*) Shade in the highest land in this area (over 150 ft.).
(*b*) Shade in the lowest land in this area (under 75 ft.).
(*c*) Measure the distance of this walk from your map.

SURVEY OF A KENT PARISH

Our journey will take us along the valley of the Stour from
Canterbury. On the banks of the Stour near a mill is indicated
on the 2½-inch map. This old water-mill is situated where there
would appear to be a break in the gradient of the river so that
the current runs strongly and where it is easy to divert a side-
stream so as to get an artificial fall to turn the mill-wheel. During
the heavy rainfall the river is still likely to flood the low-lying
ground around it. This area is known as a *flood-plain*. In 1927 the
river flooded so badly that the mill-cottage had to barricade its
front door!

1. How wide is the flood-plain here? ....
2. Are there any other houses near the river? If so, why?...........
....

....

3. What is the flood-plain used for? ....
....

....

4. Do a quick sketch to show the river, weir gate and mill.
5. How is the river water controlled?..................................
....

6. How old is the present mill?..
  As the mill is not now used it may be possible only to see some
  part of it. Try and get the idea of how such a water-mill
  worked—how each floor was used.
7. What other sources of power beside water was later used?

....

The party will be in four groups:

Group 1 will do a transect with Mr Murray across the Stour
Valley.

Group 2 will do a land-use survey using 2½-inch maps.

Pasture . . .	P	Rough pasture and heath	H
Arable . . .	A	Built-up waste land .	R
Orchards and market			
gardens . .	O		

Group 3 farm survey (see separate sheet).

VILLAGE BUILDING SURVEY

On the outline map we shall classify buildings according to use
and age. The age groupings will help us to see the original site
and nucleus of the village. It will also show us at a glance the
later areas of development. The actual shape of the village will
be of interest to us—it may give a pattern which was one of
defence—houses were often built close to the church which
itself could be a stronghold. Does Chilham look this type?

Key to Use

Houses . . .	H	Workshops . .	W
Shops . . .	S	Churches . .	C
Cafes and restaurants	R	Social centre .	Sc
Farms . . .	F	Any other building	M

DATING A HOUSE

Timber and Plaster Houses

Overhanging upper floors, fifteenth, sixteenth, or early seventeenth
century.
Uprights close together, fifteenth century.

Medieval

Few uprights, diagonal braces sixteenth- or early seventeenth-
century *Tudor*.

Brick Houses (usually red)

Elaborate doorways, panelled doors, fanlight over door, fashioned seventeenth, eighteenth, nineteenth century.

Modern Houses

Larger windows, plain design, twentieth century.

For age we can identify the survey

(*a*) Do sketches of these different types of houses and the church.
(*b*) Discover how far away the nearest urban centre for work and entertainment is. What is the means of transport? How long does it take?

....Medieval and Tudor up to seventeenth century (mainly timber and plaster)

....Seventeenth, eighteenth, nineteenth century (usually red brick if not local stone).

....Twentieth-century modern houses.

English geographers seem convinced of the value of such studies. They feel that the mind gains a truer picture of the complex working of geographical factors from the detailed study of small regions. Similarly, they are convinced that the student gets 'the truest and most vivid and intelligible picture of all from the study of a small region with which (he) himself can become familiar'.[1] It would be difficult indeed to quarrel with these assumptions, and one of the great strengths of English secondary education is the effectiveness with which geographers have been able to organize and carry out such studies.

Purely local, more limited geographical studies are carried out with equal thoroughness and attention to detail in both urban and rural environments. Students may spend considerable time investigating the geology of the area in which they live, its physical features, climate, soils, animals, natural vegetation, agricultural and/or industrial services. The results of such a study (carried out by a group of sixth formers over a two-day period) are summarized on pp. 86–87. The students divided

------

[1] *Geography and Education*. London: Ministry of Education, Pamphlet No. 29, 1962, p. 8.

their home area into ten 'regions', and then surveyed each region in terms of the factors indicated on the margin to the reader's right. Accompanying the final report were twenty student-made maps as well as considerable additional explanatory material:[1]

One is also impressed with the effort English geographers have made to put together numbers of 'sample studies' that enable the student to move from the study of the purely local and familiar (perhaps of an area dairy farm) to the study of a similar farm in say, Denmark or the United States. Such studies are designed to bring the outside world closer to children in the most realistic, detailed, and meaningful way possible— they are, in a sense, 'field studies in the classroom'.

While the Geographical Association has produced a collection of sample studies for use in the schools,[2] I found the 'Farm Study Scheme' of the Association of Agriculture[3] among the most creative approaches to the provision of this kind of material. The Association has put together (at this writing) twenty or so sample studies of real, individual 'working' farms located in various parts of the world. For example, studies are available for a tobacco farm in Rhodesia, a sheep-wheat farm in Australia a dairy farm in Canada, etc. Each 'packet' contains detailed maps of the larger region, the locality, and of the farm itself. The family who work the farm are introduced through photographs, as are the landscape, animals, and equipment. Detailed information is given concerning crops raised, problems encountered, marketing procedures, land formation, and soil, climate, etc. In addition, since these are real rather than imaginary farms, it is possible to keep in touch by letter with the farmer himself so that additional information may be obtained and the study kept up to date and alive.

American social studies teachers would be similarly impressed, I am certain, with the practice here of equipping and

[1] J. Haddon, *Local Geography*. London: George Philip and Son, Limited, 1964, pp. 86–7.
[2] *Sample Studies*. The Geographical Association. Sheffield: Park Branch Library, Duke Street, 1962.
[3] 78 Buckingham Gate, London, S.W.1.

Cross 'Plains'	Cross Hill	Cross 'Shelf'	Drained Peat Moors	Drained Alluvial Moors
10	9	8	7	6
	4 private houses	4 farmhouses, private houses, inns. Buildings mostly early nineteenth century of limestone or conglomerate Outside piping (disused) for gas, in some cases		Village of Lower Wea plus scattered farms. Buildings mainly of limestone; later additions in brick. One ro of old brick cottages.
		Cross { Farming services one-time coaching now by-passed	(Note: All village patterns linear)	Lower Weare (Bridge Settlement)
Sheep tracks	Several tracks to Hill-main on to quarry	Metalled road E.W. (Old Coach Road)	Old Coaching Road on west side runs N.S. Joins new (1924) A38 at Lower Weare and there crosses the Axe. Cross Moor Drove runs W.E. on N. Bank of River Yoe—dates from enclosure, 1778	
Water reservoir		3 inns, shop, P.O., water-works, school		1 inn, P.O., 1 shop, bed and breakfast, 1 garage
Derelict lime kiln	None	Cabinet maker, builder, water-works	One-time brewery now farm building	
Derelict limestone quarry			None	
Rough, grazing		Market gardens (mainly vegetables, strawberries) some orchards	Pastures for dairy cattle, meadow, 1 market garden	Dairying summer pasture for dairy ca a few orchards. 1 market garden
Short, tough grass, gorse and brambles			All cultivated and mostly under grass (see above)	
No surface drainage		Some wells	Artificial drainage ('Rhynes')	Rhynes divide and drain fields into Riv Yeo and Axe which meander across from E.W. Meanders in so cases straightened. Fishing in both rive

[A]xe River Terrace	Weare 'Shelf'	Nodding (or Notting) Hill	The Coombe	Sparrow Hill	
	4	3	2	1	REGIONS
	Church, vicarage, private houses, club mostly in Lias limestone	Mostly in Lias limestone, 4 farms (inc. 17 barns) a few cottages, 1 bungalow	Modernized farmhouse	1 farmhouse, 1 large W.D. Depot, 2 bungalows, 1 derelict Chapel	BUILDINGS
[W]eare [F]arming [Se]ttlement)					VILLAGES
	Narrow road E.W. along shelf		1 metalled road connecting villages. Difficult track		COMMUNICATIONS
	Church, men's club, school			Piped water-supply to fields	SERVICES
		None		Disused windmill now farmhouse	INDUSTRIES
[pa]sture and [l]ittle [ar]able [fo]dder [cro]ps)	Gardens, pasture, orchard	Dairying	Too steep for use	Dairying-breeding dairy cattle. Some arable (fodder crops)	AGRICULTURE
					VEGETATION
					MINERALS
[So]me wells	Little surface water. Some streams run into the Coombe		Main stream. Small but deeply in-cised	Some ponds and wells	DRAINAGE

reserving a particular room for the teaching of geography. They would be equally impressed with the quality and quantity of materials contained in such rooms—the varieties of maps of all scales and styles, meteorological instruments, reference materials including almanacs, rail, sea, and air time-tables, air photos, periodicals and yearbooks.

Sixth form work in geography exhibits most of the positive (and, of course, some of the negative) features we have come to associate with sixth form work in general in England. In many ways sixth form teaching would be comparable to college level work in the United States. Students use a variety of texts, monographs, journal articles, and other sources, work more on their own, and deal with ideas and techniques that are considered 'inappropriate' for younger pupils. For example, a group of sixth formers I observed at Guildford Royal Grammar School were pursuing a two-year course including map studies, statistical cartography, considerable attention to geomorphology, a study of western Europe in great detail, and a period of concentrated study at a field center. During a class session (there were nine students in the group) they were in the process of investigating agricultural problems along the Rhone in France, and they were using (among other sources) a great variety of related, short, journal articles, clippings from periodicals and newspapers, etc., to aid in their search for relevant data.

One might include a number of other notable and positive developments—for example, the creation of courses in literary geography such as the one offered at De Burgh Comprehensive School in Surrey, in which students examine a series of books like Alan Paton's *Cry the Beloved Country* for their geographical implications; the great variety of local and continental touring undertaken by secondary schools of all kinds that are, of course, taken advantage of (and often sponsored by) geography departments; and, in general, the positive, more flexible, less tradition dominated attitude that many geographers seem to hold concerning the role of geography in the schools. This is often the subject in which teachers are most likely (in my experience) to consider a problem or question that is *not* in the syllabus; to range outside of geography as such and to include material dealing with economic, social, and even political problems; to deal with current questions and issues that may be of real concern to their students. In short, it is the geographers who have made the most determined effort to broaden the scope and increase the relevance of their curricular offerings, and their contributions towards helping thousands of English secondary school children to better understand twentieth-century man and society cannot be underestimated.

It would be both unfair and dishonest if our assessment of geography were to end on this purely positive note. A number of problems and questions occurred to me as I observed children, visited with teachers, and studied curriculum guides, syllabuses, and other related materials. One of the most significant of these can best be illustrated through the recounting of a particular classroom visit.

The incident I have in mind involved a group of thirty-three fourth form boys in a large secondary modern school. They were about fourteen-years-old, and all were planning to become 'school leavers' at the earliest opportunity. (They were, of course, in the lowest stream in this particular school.) As I sat down to observe the lesson, the boys kept up a constant chatter. Pens and pencils were tossed about the room, the teacher was largely ignored, or when not, treated quite rudely—often with a mock, sarcastic twist to the typically English 'Sir' that so often precedes or concludes an English student's verbal communications with his teacher. For his part, the teacher ignored all of this, sat on the edge of a desk and read aloud out of a geography book dealing with farming, addressing himself to the two or three boys who were, apparently, listening. Later he confided to me that he tries to talk about things like farming, trucking, etc. because 'boys like this aren't interested in anything else'. The textbook itself could have been appropriate for eleven-year-olds—but it most certainly was not mature enough for these boys, who, I am certain, were quite well aware of the book's inadequacies in this regard. The teacher droned on and the class went from bad to worse until I decided to leave to avoid further embarrassment for the teacher and for myself.

Now, none of this suggests that farming *per se* is an inappropriate study for these boys—nor that with some reasonable attention to teaching method, this teacher might not have improved the situation. I think rather, that this observation symbolizes a very real danger in English education (and in American education as well) that may, unfortunately, have been given a push by the influential Newsom Report. It seems to me that the Report leaves itself open to anti-intellectual interpretations that may well result in the creation of courses of study that are, to be sure, 'relevant'—yet possibly far less liberalizing, far less worthy of study, and perhaps far less significant in terms of helping children understand the social and physical world in which they find themselves. As I examine new and old geography syllabuses for 'non-academic', 'Newsom' children, I am impressed too often with their tendency to avoid what may seem to be overly complicated (yet vital) ideas; to tend towards the narrowly 'practical'; in short, to risk emasculating the geography curriculum for the sake of unproven assumptions about such children's capacities for understanding.

Lawrence Cremin has said that the great challenge facing American educators today is to 'design up-to-date curricula that make no compromise with truth or significance and yet prove attractive and comprehensible to dull or poorly motivated children'.[1] This seems to me to be an equally challenging problem for English educators—particularly in the social studies.

In the section on primary education we referred to newer techniques (in this case the creation of a 'hunting game') that may help both American and English educators to achieve this objective. No one suggests that this one example was in any way adequate; nevertheless, I tried to make the point that there might be dozens of unconventional approaches that could conceivably help us to move towards that ideal situation in which (as Bruner put it) 'any subject can be taught effectively in some intellectually honest form to any child at any stage of development'.[2]

Let me suggest a similar possibility in geography. Suppose

[1] L. Cremin, *The Genius of American Education*. Pittsburgh: The University of Pittsburgh Press, 1965, p. 62.

[2] J. Bruner, *The Process of Education*. New York: Vintage Books, 1963, p. 33.

for example, a group of geographers engaged in syllabus construction could agree that one of the ideas of 'worth' and 'significance'—one of geography's more important insights—had to do with the notion that a place's relative location or 'situation' has become increasingly important as man's relationship to man has become so; that places no longer exist in isolation. *If* the geographers in question (and I fully recognize that this is a very big 'if' indeed) accepted this generalization they might attempt to develop what could be an exceedingly 'concrete', highly visual 'model of reality' that might help clarify it. For example, . . . a secondary school teacher might outline a hypothetical place called 'Newland' on the blackboard. Newland is rectangularly shaped: its length is 200 miles, its width 25 miles. It is a physically homogeneous area, with equal amounts of rainfall, similar temperature range, and soil conditions that are ideal for the production of cotton. The same level of technology exists throughout Newland, and its people share the same values, beliefs and attitudes. At one end of this rectangular land is a factory that manufactures cloth out of raw cotton. Its sole source of cotton is the hinterland farms of Newland. In order to earn dividends for its owners, the factory can afford to pay the farmers £2 per bale of cotton.

Running the length of Newland (and through its middle) is a railroad. It charges 8s for transporting a bale of cotton fifty miles. It costs Newland's farmers £1 to raise a bale of cotton.

Having sketched Newland, its factory, and its railroad on the blackboard and recorded the date given above, the teacher might suggest that the class formulate some hypotheses about the possible ways in which Newland's farmers would use their land. It should be clear, for example, that a farmer 200 miles from the factory would lose money if he raised and shipped cotton to the factory. He might have to turn to subsistence farming, even though his land is similar in every way to the farms located within fifty miles of the factory. Next the teacher might suggest that we change certain conditions and see what effect this might have on land use. What would happen if transportation costs were to go up 8s per bale per fifty miles? If the factory had to lower its price to 24s per bale?

If a cheaper method of transportation were suddenly introduced? If the demand for cotton went down and the factory closed its doors?[1]

As with the 'games' example, I can offer no guarantee that such techniques would in fact 'work'; nevertheless, the dual tasks of analyzing a discipline for conceptual priorities and then attempting to develop truly creative, imaginative, perhaps untried teaching procedures to help *most* children grasp them at some level of understanding seem to me to be as necessary here as they are in the United States.

A second point of concern might also be illustrated through a school experience—this time in an illustrious girls' grammar school. The girls (a class of fourteen fourth-formers) were studying aspects of physical geography, and their teacher was showing them a set of color slides or transparencies of the Alps, explaining the path taken by a particular glacier. The girls dutifully made illustrative drawings in their ever-present notebooks and the lesson proceeded uneventfully. Following this I talked with the teacher about her teaching methods and her syllabus and raised a question about a phrase she had used which indicated that the class eventually studies the way in which the life of the people of Norway is 'determined' by Norway's physical environment. I asked her whether she had intended to use a word as strong as 'determined', and she answered that, in her opinion, 'it was entirely appropriate'. She really didn't see the importance of the concept of 'culture' in this instance and considered it 'not relevant' to the course.

This may well be an exaggerated instance; my reporting of it, however, is not. I found something like this attitude reflected in the printed syllabuses and actual teaching procedures of many schools and teachers. This tendency towards determinism in English geography teaching (particularly at pre-sixth-form

---

[1] This is a technique I have used successfully with children of average ability. It (and many similar ideas) is described in the chapter on teaching methods written by myself and Professor R. H. Muessig in *Geography: Its Scope and Spirit*, by J. Broek. This is one of six volumes in the Social Science Seminar Series, published in 1966 by Charles E. Merrill Books, Inc., Columbus, Ohio, and edited by R. H. Muessig and V. Rogers.

levels) has been recognized by a number of English writers,[1] and I have no intention of dwelling upon it here. Nevertheless, English readers in particular might consider these comments by an American geographer concerning an area often studied in both American and English schools—Latin America. These excerpts come from a section entitled, 'That "Impossible" Environment':[2]

And then there is that other grand daddy of a latino myth which often comes to haunt geographers. This is, of course, the old rationalization which suggests that, in most of Latin America, the physical drawbacks of the land pose an almost insurmountable barrier to economic development and a more uniform distribution of population. For many (including some geographers) this seems to be a valid assumption, but for others, it smacks of a facile explanation based on skimpy knowledge and age-old prejudices.

Viewed objectively, the picture of man-land relations in Latin America appears to be a composite of anomalies. On the one hand, it is known that: (1) the rapidly increasing population tends to be concentrated within a few hundred miles of the sea, leaving considerable empty or thinly settled areas to the interior (especially in South America); and (2) the gross pattern of population distribution is characterized by what James has called a 'hollow' frontier. On the other hand, it is obvious that the expanding population is not effectively occupying the empty lands; and worse, there is an artificial country-to-town movement which is depleting the countryside of what is often badly needed labor while it creates slums and swells unemployment in the cities. As an added joker to this anomalous set of conditions, some people insist that agrarian reform is one of the absolute 'musts' to meet the revolution of rising expectations and the threat of Communism in rural Latin America.

If one poses the question—'why not seriously investigate the possibilities of large-scale occupance of the lightly settled interior

---

[1] See, for example, S. R. Eyre, 'Determinism and the Ecological Approach to Geography', *Geography*, Volume XLIX, November 1964, pp. 369—76, or E. C. Marchant, 'Geography in Education in England and Wales', *Geography*, Volume XLIX, July 1964, pp. 185–6, or *Geography and Education*, Ministry of Education Pamphlet No. 29, London: Her Majesty's Stationery Office, 1962, p. 30.

[2] J. P. Augelli, 'A Controversial Image of Latin America: A Geographer's View', *Journal of Geography*, Volume 62, March 1963, pp. 105–6.

lands?', the stock answer is likely to be—'these lands are too hot, too wet, too dry, too isolated, too inconvenient', etc. Moreover, why bother with such prosaic approaches when one can dream of spectacular solutions like agrarian reform, industrialization and the like.

This argument of environmental impossibility reminds some geographers of that old wives' tale in United States history known as the 'Great American Desert'. Frontiersmen, emerging from the humid eastern forests and carrying with them their typical European distrust of new and untried environmental conditions, jumped at an unwarranted conclusion when they gazed upon the great grasslands of North America. 'Any land that won't grow trees won't grow crops', they claimed. But experimentation and adaptation soon proved them wrong, and today this same 'Great American Desert' is one of the world's great producers of cereals and meats.

Is it conceivable that our present negative conclusions *vis-a-vis* 'the green hell' of the Amazon Basin, for instance, are equally false? We do not really know because we have found it more convenient to let prejudices determine judgment rather than expend the effort and capital to arrive at a rational conclusion. There are at least four Japanese agricultural colonies that refused to be discouraged by the 'green hell' of the Amazon. After only a few decades of effort, these settlements loom as striking successes. They produce the bulk of their own food with a surplus for sale, and they have found convenient cash crops in the form of black pepper and jute. The conclusion appears inescapable that among the many obstacles to economic development in rural Latin America is a built-in prejudice against (and an abysmal ignorance of) the potential of untried environments, especially tropical environments.

Closely related to the problem of determinism is the tendency to emphasize a narrow, descriptive approach in the study of other people and places—even though there is more effort made to broaden such studies among geographers than there is among historians. Again, perhaps, an example will serve to clarify the point. The following material is taken from a sample study published by the Geographical Association. The study is concerned with cotton raising on a farm in the Gezira area of Sudan. It is in many ways an excellent collection of climatic, physical, and other data. Included (in an attempt, I presume, to add a human factor to the study) is this description of the life-ways of a Sudanese family.

> Siddig's busiest time is during the cotton sowing period. His children help him as much as possible but Siddig's working day occupies all the daylight hours, roughly from 6.0 a.m. to 6.0 p.m. He rides out on his donkey from his neat brick-built house in Wad Rawag early in the morning and works till about 9.0 a.m. when he has a breakfast consisting of kisr, a thin wafer made of dura, and some well-spiced meat, perhaps washed down by milk or water. The latter has to be taken from the communal well in the village as its irrigation water is contaminated by the animals. Siddig works until 6.0 p.m. with a short break for a meal, similar to his breakfast, at 2.0 p.m. For his supper he will probably have a stew consisting of meat and vegetables, together with kisr and milk.

> In contrast to his busy sowing period, Siddig has a good deal of leisure time from the end of April to the beginning of July. Most of his time then is spent resting on his bed, a wooden frame with interwoven goat-skin thongs, or squatting in the shade talking to his friends. They drink tea flavoured with mint and very sweet black coffee.[1]

It seems to me that there are very real dangers here in describing a pattern of life so different from one's own without any attention to certain anthropological or sociological understandings. For example, it is important to approach the study of a culture that is strikingly different from one's own with at least some understanding of the fact that most important differences in human behavior can be explained in terms of *learned* patterns of social behavior rather than as differences in biological apparatus or other genetically inherited mechanisms. Similarly, one ought to have some notion of how one's own experiences are influenced by one's cultural heritage—to recognize that most men tend to view their own way of life as the most reasonable and natural. It would be equally important to recognize that *every* cultural system is logical and coherent in its own terms—that all of them 'make sense', given the basic assumptions and knowledge available to the specific community.

---

[1] R. C. Honeybone, 'Cotton Farm in the Gezira', *Sample Studies*. Sheffield: The Geographical Association, Park Branch Library, Duke Street, 1962, p. 32.

In other words without some attention to what might broadly be called the 'culture concept', such descriptive facts as 'Siddig spends a good deal of his time resting in his bed' or 'squatting in the shade' can be perceived in an entirely negative way, and the geography program may *reinforce* ethnocentric tendencies rather than counteract them.

This is not to suggest that geography can not be used as a vehicle for the teaching of such concepts and generalizations; it can (and, in all fairness, a number of teachers *do* deal with such ideas in their teaching). However, this is by no means the 'typical' approach, and I doubt very much if such ideas will be dealt with generally until they are *systematically* incorporated into geography (or other) syllabuses.

Similarly, one wonders why so many English geography teachers are willing to settle for narrowly physical, descriptive (although obviously thorough and rigorous) approaches to local studies. One sees a great deal of attention paid to the cataloguing of village services, but little to their evaluation; some attention to the *form* of local government but little to its effectiveness; considerable attention to 'change-over-time' but little to whether such change seems 'bad' or 'good' and why this may be so.

Perhaps all of this is related to what some critics perceive of as a lack of balance in English geography syllabuses. Possibly because of the traditional inclusion here in geography of a good deal of what would, in America, be classified as geology, there does seem to be a general over-emphasis on the physical and, of course (unavoidably) a neglect of the human. This seems true at all levels of education, from primary school to college or university. (On the other hand, English geographers might well wonder about the absence of so much that they hold dear, were they to examine a sampling of American geography or social studies syllabuses!) Perhaps once again the argument boils down to one of priorities in education, with American educators viewing the contributions of human geography as more likely to help the average citizen understand the world in which he lives and therefore emphasizing that aspect of the discipline—though surely not neglecting completely the physical. English geographers seem to hold the opposite view, and if one adds to this the fact that geography (after the fourth or fifth form) is largely an optional course that is taken more with a view towards preparing a future *geographer* rather than a future 'citizen', these differences in emphasis become somewhat clearer.

One might, if space permitted, discuss more fully what seemed to me to be the very real problems of overlap between primary school and the early years of secondary school as well as the considerable overlap that seems to exist between work done in the sixth form and that carried out in college or university.[1] Or, one might dwell on the tendencies of geographers (as well as historians) to conceive of the sixth form as a 'dividing line'—a place where students begin to *use* knowledge as well as *acquire* it, to be finally allowed into the inner sanctum of geographical ideas that are somehow considered inappropriate for those below this intellectual 'iron curtain'. For the moment, however, this brief treatment must suffice.

Undoubtedly, some of this criticism is more valid than the rest, and of course, many exceptions to my generalizations exist, both among schools in general and surely among individual teachers. Nevertheless, these seem to me to be the salient points about which discussion might most profitably center.

[1] This problem, too, has been discussed at length by English Educators. See, for example, The Geographical Association's Supplementary Paper No. 1 (November 1962) dealing with the overlap between sixth form and university courses in geography. Obtainable from the Geographical Association, Park Branch Library, Duke Street, Sheffield

V: SOCIAL STUDIES AS A SCHOOL SUBJECT

MOST HISTORIANS are fond of pointing out to their uninitiated, 'lay' friends that history does not necessarily repeat itself. However, at this point in time—approximately twenty years after the passage of the Education Act of 1944—we find some striking historical parallels that need to be explored more fully. The reader will recall that it was in 1944, when it was decided to raise the school-leaving age to fifteen, that advocates of social studies courses for secondary schools reached the peak of their enthusiasm. Conditions were ripe for something new—for fresh solutions to unique problems. Social studies as a school subject seemed about to come into its own until a host of unforeseen problems (as well as a series of strategic errors on the part of social studies supporters) brought the movement to a halt. The reader may further recall that we ended our treatment of the historical development of social studies as a school subject on a hopeful note, listing a number of events that set the stage for a possible 'second chance' for social studies in England. Among the most important of these, of course, was the Department of Education and Science's decision to raise the school-leaving age to sixteen. Headmasters, teachers, and local Education Authority officials are now faced (as in 1944) with the prospect of considerably increased numbers of so-called 'non-academic' children continuing on in secondary schools—and again the call goes out for more interesting, practical, and relevant courses of study for them.

Conditions in 1944 and in the 1960's are, of course, different in hundreds of ways, and our historical parallel breaks down rather quickly if one pushes the comparison too far. Nevertheless, those interested in fostering the cause of broadly integrated, cross-disciplinary studies of men and society in English secondary schools are faced currently with many of the same questions, dilemmas and decisions as were their counterparts in 1944. Whether or not they will adopt the same strategies and, perhaps, make some of the same mistakes of course remains to be seen. At the moment, there appear to be a number of positive signs on the horizon—as well as an almost frightening, certainly discouraging number of 1944-like approaches that can most charitably be described as re-treads of ideas that were tried and found wanting two decades ago. Let us first examine the positive.

Dr James L. Henderson, Senior Lecturer in the Teaching of History and International Affairs at the London University Institute of Education and one of England's most outspoken critics of narrowly conceived school history syllabuses, has become an impassioned advocate of the need for greater 'synthesis' in history offerings—the need for 'composite, modern studies' comprising 'aspects' of history, geography, anthropology, sociology, and psychology, as well as other subjects. He argues as well for the adoption of 'common curriculums' for all eleven- to fifteen-year-old children, as well as 'thematically' organized courses.[1] Henderson's position tends to balance somewhat the objections to 'synthesized' studies so articulately expressed by his colleague at the London Institute, W. H. Burston.[2]

The following syllabus is, perhaps, illustrative of the sort of program that Henderson has encouraged. It is a two-year course, intended to take the place of traditional offerings in history and geography:

1. MAN IN SOCIETY: HIS WAYS OF LIFE AND WORK

The Social, Economic, Industrial, Scientific, Artistic, and Cultural Aspects of the Modern World

(1) The shrinking world.
    (i) Transport developments and their impact.
    (ii) Inter-personal communications—postal services, tele-communications, radio, etc.—and their impact.
    (iii) Economic interdependence—the individual and sources of supply—expansion of world trade.

---

[1] See *The Living World*, University of Sheffield Institute of Education, 1965. This booklet contains an essay by Dr. Henderson as well as sample syllabuses and other pertinent material.

[2] See pages 16, 68 for a fuller treatment of W. H. Burston's position.

(2) Twentieth-century achievements and their implications.
    (i) The fight against disease.
    (ii) The expanding universe—man reaches outwards.
    (iii) Spreading of literacy.
    (iv) Man's increasing leisure.
    (v) Improvements in working life.
    (vi) Personal freedom—to live and work without fear.
    (vii) Food and health.
    (viii) Control over natural resources.
    (ix) Increased knowledge of the physical world.
    (x) The status of women.
    (xi) The rights of the child.

(3) The business of government.
    (i) The purpose of government—an ordered framework for social life.
    (ii) The functions of government—protecting the citizen, regulation of trade, social welfare, provision for social growth, laws and their administration, finance, relationships with other lands.
    (iii) Government by consent—elections (local and national) in Britain. Comparison of this system with the systems of other countries.
    (iv) The nation's finances, budgets, taxes and rates.
    (v) The idea of sovereignty—the province of government. Individual and State. State and State.
    (vi) Relations between governments—diplomatic and consular services—passports—the subject abroad—extradition.

(4) Man's work and wages.
    (i) The function of money.
    (ii) Industries—large and small.
    (iii) Wages and profits.
    (iv) Management and men.

(5) The importance of design.
    (i) Design and health.
    (ii) Design and safety.
    (iii) Design and efficiency.

(6) The importance of leisure.
    (i) How a community cares for its leisure.
    (ii) The place of sport, art, music, theatre, cinema, etc., in the community.
    (iii) The press, radio and television.

2. THE WORLD'S PEOPLES: THEIR PROBLEMS AND PROSPECTS

(1) The meaning of 'development'.
> (i) The more developed countries:
> > (a) Characteristics: high standard of living. Widespread education—through State system. Relatively mobile social structure. High level of employment. Exploitation of natural resources. Community health programme and precautions. Large export/import trade.
> > (b) Problems: need to find overseas markets. Often need to import raw materials for industry.
> (ii) The less-developed countries:
> > (a) Characteristics: Poverty. Ignorance. Disease. Hunger. Static social structure. Inadequate exploitation of resources. Few exports.
> > (b) Needs: Foreign investment. Assistance in developing educational programmes. Improvement in medical services. Attack on major diseases. Improvement in food production techniques. Development of government and administration.
>
> (*N.B.*—It is suggested that this section can be most conveniently organized by a simultaneous study of two regions of the world, one within Europe and the other in, perhaps, West Africa or South America.)

(2) The desire for self-government.
> (i) Reasons for this:
> > (a) Desire to imitate more advance countries.
> > (b) Dissatisfaction with colonial regime.
> > (c) Desire to improve social conditions.
> > (d) Consciousness of a 'national' unity.
> (ii) Problems of transition.
> > (a) Leadership and organization of nationalist movements.
> > (b) General problems of preparation—economic, administrative, etc.
> > (c) Problems of unification-language (see section 5), customs, tribal divisions, regionalism.
> (iii) Newly independent countries.
> > (a) Political machinery.
> > (b) Political affiliations.
> > (c) Development of resources.
> > (d) Education and Social Services.

(*N.B.*—The subject matter is intended to be brought out by a study of three countries. The first two of which will show the main features of the movement towards independence and self-government. Thus, Nigeria would be our own selection as a country illustrating this movement in a situation where careful preparation was made for the achievement of independence, and the Congo being selected as illustrating the results of lack of preparation.

India would be our choice as the region around which to centre the third topic in order to give an example of a country's progress since its achievement of independence and the problems which it has faced and has still to face.)

(3) Technical assistance—nature and achievements.
    (i) Sources and reasons.
        (*a*) Attitude of more developed countries towards less developed.
        (*b*) The facts of mutual benefit.
        (*c*) Aid from individual governments.
        (*d*) Mutual help within the Commonwealth.
        (*e*) Assistance through international organizations. United Nations and Agencies.
    (ii) Nature of technical assistance work.
        (*a*) Designed not just to solve problems for countries, but to help them solve their own problems and achieve a position in which they are able to solve their own problems in future without outside assistance.
        (*b*) Rarely possible to tackle problems in isolation—normally, attack on problems of less-developed areas is a many-sided attack involving co-operation between various specialist organizations.
        (*c*) Conditions under which assistance is provided—guarantees of rights of countries to ask for assistance and to prepare themselves to receive it. Any money received is in form of a loan.
    (iii) The achievements so far.
    A study of technical assistance work undertaken both in and by the five regions studied in this part of the syllabus.

(4) The world's religions.
    (*N.B.*—The religions actually studied in this section would be chosen by reference to the countries or regions selected in the foregoing sections.)

(5) Language, languages, and dialects.
    (i) The nature of language.
    (ii) Languages.
    (iii) Dialects.
    (iv) Language as a problem in development.
    (v) The study of a foreign language.
    (*N.B.*—The European language being studied or which it is proposed to study would naturally influence the choice of the European country to be studied under section (i) above or, perhaps more properly, the country chosen would determine the language.)

3. THE WORLD OF THE TWENTIETH CENTURY: ITS HISTORICAL BACKGROUND AND ITS PRESENT PROBLEMS

(1) The idea of society.
    (i) Purposes.
    (ii) Rights and responsibilities.

(2) The idea of a nation.
    (i) Characteristics.
    (ii) Sources of authority.
    (iii) National differences—to understand is to value.

(3) States in the twentieth century—problems of preservation and extension. The origins and historical development of:
    (i) Democracy.
    (ii) Socialism.
    (iii) Communism.
    (iv) Nazism.
    (v) Facism.

(4) Relations between States.
    (i) Balance of power.
    (ii) Search for markets.
    (iii) Forms of diplomacy.
    (iv) Extension of power and influence.
    (v) Joint economic organizations.
    (vi) Regional security arrangements.

(5) War—its causes and results.
    (i) World War I.
    (ii) World War II.
    (iii) Some recent threats to peace.
    (iv) The Cold War.

(6) Revolutions and their impact.

(7) Instruments of peace in the modern world.
    (i) The League of Nations.
    (ii) United Nations Organization—the structure and function of the General Assembly, Security Council, U.N.E.F., International Court, etc.
    (iii) The powers of international organizations—the sovereign rights of member states.

(8) Ideals of the modern world—the Universal Declaration of Human Rights—origin, content, the present situation.

(9) Some obstacles to progress.
    (i) Political rivalry.
    (ii) Poverty and wealth.
    (iii) Competition for power.
    (iv) The will and the way.

(10) Varying responsibilities.
    (i) The individual.
    (ii) The State.
    (iii) Organization of States.[1]

Similarly, a band of devoted, hard-working teachers at London's famed Kidbrooke School has been working incessantly to develop effective, lively social studies courses—courses that go far beyond the practically oriented, locally confining syllabuses so typical of 1944. Kidbrooke's courses are firmly rooted in the vocabulary, concepts, and methods of the social sciences. They are *not* geared exclusively to 'non-academic' children, and they are at least as rigorous and demanding as are the more or less typical history and geography offerings generally taught to children at this age level. Without attempting a thorough description of the specific syllabuses currently being taught at Kidbrooke, it seems especially important to mention that *all* students take

[1] *The Living Past.* University of Sheffield Institute of Education, 1965, pp. 34–40.

a social science-humanities course (developed by the Kidbrooke faculty) during their first three years. Ultimately, students may elect to do both O and A level work in economics, as well as A level work in sociology. By the time this is published Kidbrooke girls will also be able to take the O level social science course now being developed by the Associated Examining Board as well as the Metropolitan C.S.E. social studies syllabus. Non-social scientists in the sixth form may elect to take 'Introduction to the Social Sciences' as part of their minority time, and plans are under way to offer (eventually) a composite A level course in the social sciences.

Kidbrooke's faculty, incidentally, is anything but convinced that the social science syllabuses of the various examining boards are beyond criticism. On the contrary, they spent a great deal of time pointing out a number of their faults during my visit to the school. However, they seemed determined *not* to repeat the mistakes of earlier social studies advocates who rather naïvely sought acceptance of their subject on an entirely non-examined basis. They feel strongly that, so long as the examination system remains an integral part of English education (and it shows little sign of any significant decline at this writing), social studies will have to follow to some extent the examination pattern of other, older, more accepted subjects. This, they reason, is the most logical means of gaining academic respectability for social studies and the social sciences.

The development of C.S.E. syllabuses in social studies needs to be mentioned at once as a positive factor in terms of encouraging and enabling many schools to move rather quickly into the social studies area. Yet, the fact that the C.S.E. is (theoretically, at least) less demanding—less 'rigorous'—less 'academic' than the G.C.E. may ultimately do social studies more harm than good. As has been said before, the chances for the general acceptance of a course associated with the non-academic child in England, are at the very least, somewhat limited.

It is exceedingly difficult, incidentally, to generalize about the C.S.E. syllabuses in social studies. They are, of course, new, and most are in a state of continuing revision. Some seem more promising than others. All consist essentially of listings of *topics* for study, and thematic or conceptual approaches are non-existent. There are portions of various courses that are indeed, social science oriented and lend themselves to a fuller exploration and understanding of some of the ideas, questions and work-ways that have emerged through the years from disciplines such as anthropology, sociology, and economics. Much time is devoted in virtually all of the syllabuses I examined, however, to topics that are at best on the periphery of social science; topics that are 'community service' or 'practically' oriented, e.g., 'understanding banking and insurance', 'how to budget', 'preventing accidents in the home', 'helping the handicapped or aged', etc.

In any event, the ultimate impact of the new C.S.E. syllabuses will simply have to be judged at a later date; at the moment, their acceptance and influence remain uncertain.

Perhaps one of the most refreshing approaches to the study of man and society in secondary schools is currently in the process of development at London's St Dunstan's College—a large, independent boys' school with a reputation for academic excellence. St Dunstan's is good enough to dare to be different, and its headmaster is, apparently, willing to allow his less complacent faculty members to experiment with a variety of new ideas.

St Dunstan's middle school (including boys aged thirteen to sixteen) is, at this writing, offering a new social studies course for virtually all of its students. The only pupils excluded are (for a change!) the 'duller' boys who will need O level passes in history and geography. The vast majority will take social studies for four years, by-pass O levels in history and geography and go on to the sixth form. In essence, the St Dunstan's social studies course is *not* then, tied to external examinations; therefore it can range both widely and deeply in search of challenging topics for study. Similarly, since all but the *slower* students are included in the course, and since it is taught by established members of the geography and history departments who have gotten together and 'pooled' their talents, it has something of a headstart in conquering (on a local level, at least) the 'prestige' or acceptance problem referred to earlier. While the syllabus itself is flexible and, quite purposely rather sketchy, the following description should give the reader some idea of the nature of the course.

To begin with, ancient and medieval history are excluded since, as the syllabus states, 'priorities lie elsewhere'. Third formers begin with a study of what is essentially the economic geography of Britain in the twentieth century. Problems related to population growth and distribution, the development of power resources, farming and its relationship to natural (and national) needs, etc. are studied, as well as topics dealing with the growth of the idea of democracy and problems of contemporary Britain (political, sociological, and economic in particular).

Fourth formers study the growth and development of modern Europe, including such topics as colonialism and political ideologies as well as a brief history of the United States and its emergence as a world power.

The fifth form consists of an attempt to compare less familiar societies possessing 'widely different cultural patterns from those of Western Europe'. Both contemporary China and Russia are studied in some depth, as is 'Africa in the Twentieth Century'. Finally the course concludes with a study of the 'Makers of Modern Society', e.g., Freud, Mazzini, Darwin, Henry Ford and others.

No one at St Dunstan's feels that the social studies course is in anything approaching final form; drastic changes will still be made and the syllabus may never be finally and permanently 'complete'. Nevertheless, it does represent a unique contribution to the social studies arsenal, and the fact that it exists at a school like St Dunstan's (and for its *brighter* boys at that) may be a persuasive argument for others who are contemplating similar changes.

Another prestigious boys' school is carrying out a somewhat similar program. I refer to Sevenoaks, the dynamic pace-setting institution to which we turned earlier for an example of excellence in sixth-form teaching.

Its history and geography masters have developed a course that may eventually include *all* boys at Sevenoaks, eleven through eighteen. It is referred to as 'P.E.B.', i.e., Precedent, Experience and Belief. The course is expected to take the place of conventional history and geography offerings, and (eventually) to eliminate the existing general studies course now given in the sixth form. During 'O Level Year', i.e., the fifth form, the P.E.B. curriculum would be close enough to the standard O level syllabuses in history and geography so that Sevenoaks students may take the exams if they wish. Ultimately, however, the staff would like to see P.E.B. culminate in an A level examination taken by everyone.

Currently, P.E.B. is being offered experimentally during years one, two and three, ages eleven to fourteen. The course is chronologically organized, and attempts to deal simultaneously with the physical and human problems involved in the development of man and society. First-year students study the origins of the Earth, simple geology and related aspects of evolution, primitive tribes, the 'fertile crescent' and the Greeks. Second-year boys work within the theme of 'The Expanding World', studying topics such as 'Settlements and Communications', 'The Growing of Crops', 'Life in India and China', etc. 'The Growth of Society' is the theme for year three, and 'New Ideas about the Universe', 'Renaissance and Discovery', 'Climate and Man', etc. are typical areas of study. The tentative theme for the fourth year is 'The Shrinking World', although specific, illustrative topics had not been developed at this writing.

Again, one must emphasize the tentativeness of such outlines —the flexibility that is implied and the range of investigation that is encouraged. Sevenoaks, along with a number of other schools, is breaking new ground, and 'final answers' are simply not yet (and perhaps ought not to be) available.

Perhaps one of the most thorough and creatively designed examples of 'the new social studies' in England is the program developed under the direction of C. J. Hetherington, Headmaster at Kibworth School in Leicestershire. Kibworth is non-selective, taking all area children regardless of ability at the age of eleven plus, and keeping them until age fourteen. At that time Kibworth's children leave 'middle' school and proceed automatically to a much larger 'upper' school where they may, if they wish, continue their education. (Many children, of course, elect to drop out of school at fifteen and do not attend the 'upper' school.)

One of the problems that the Headmaster and his staff faced, then, was creating the kind of school which would make the transition years between primary and upper school less abrupt, academically meaningful and intellectually challenging for *all* of Kibworth's children. This led, among other things, to an unstreamed first year (the Head hopes to have the entire school unstreamed eventually) and to a drastic reappraisal of the adequacy of existing curricular patterns.

Ultimately, it was decided to create a social studies curriculum that would emphasize *individual* rather than class learning —a curriculum that would replace traditional history and geography courses—a curriculum that would combine the talents of a *team* of teachers—and, finally, a curriculum organized in terms of broad, interdisciplinary 'themes' rather than narrow, fact-saturated topics.

At this writing, the course for the first year has been developed and is being tried out in the classroom. The basic theme is 'Mankind in the Making', and five sub-topics comprise the essential areas of study for the year. These are:

> Man's Beginnings.
> Man the Toolmaker.
> Man the Farmer.
> Man the Artist.
> Man the Communicator.

The children are divided and sub-divided into groups of various sizes for differing acitivities; ample use is made of tapes, films, slides, etc. However, the heart of the program (and, I think, its truly creative and unique aspect) is the individualized study carried out through the study booklets created by Mr Hetherington and his staff. About four-fifths of the student's time is spent working on carefully graded assignments outlined in the booklets—all under the guidance of a member of the teaching team. Children are free, however, to choose particular topics for study, select varying sources of information, and to proceed at a pace which suits their abilities.

It would be physically impossible to give the reader an adequate description of the Kibworth course. However, a few examples may at least provide an insight into the nature of the teaching and learning procedures that are usually followed.

Let us imagine, then, that the children are about to embark upon a study of theme No. 3, 'Man the Farmer'. The whole group would probably be brought together for a 'general', stage-setting lecture, featuring, perhaps, appropriate films, tapes or other teaching aids that might help to make this introductory presentation especially stimulating. Following initial, small-group discussion, each student would examine carefully his personal booklet or study guide on this topic. He would find that it was divided into five sub-topics, including 'Man and Water', 'Winds and Weather', 'Rivers and Valleys', 'The Beginnings of Civilization', and 'Farmers in Temperate Lands'. Each sub-topic consists of a series of perhaps nine or ten graded assignments similar to the following:

MAN THE FARMER

Man and Water

A Visit to a Desert Sheik, I:
A Nomad's Life

SOME BOOKS TO USE:
Travel Talks (B.B.C.), Summer 1961, pp. 12, 13.
Lands in the Desert: the Middle East, pp. 1–8.

YOUR ASSIGNMENT
You are the Bedoin (or Bedawin) sheik in the picture at the bottom of p. 13 in *Travel Talks*. An English oil company engineer is coming to visit you, and you are discussing with the other men what you think he will ask about. Try to give the answers to these questions:

1. Why don't you build houses, and use tables and chairs?
2. The land around here is very bare. What wild animals are there? Do you hunt a lot for your living?
3. Why is there very little grass here? Do you grow crops to give yourselves food?
4. You and your people wear a lot of clothes. Isn't it very hot for you in this desert?
5. I saw your men riding their camels. Are the camels of any other use to you?

A Visit to a Desert Sheik, II:
The Oasis Dwellers

The oil engineer has spent the night at an *oasis* city. Before setting out in his Land Rover to find the sheik he talks to a farmer selling dates in the market. What answers might be given to these questions:

1. Do you often see the sheik and his people? Why do they come here?
2. What kind of produce are usually sold in this market?
3. Where and how are these things grown?
4. Why is it possible for folk to live and build a city here, in the middle of a desert?
5. Do you think you live a better life than the nomads?

SOME USEFUL BOOKS
Lands in the Desert: the Middle East, pp. 1–12.
Britain and Overseas, Chapter XI.
(Remember that there are many other helpful books, especially in the Library.)

The child may then proceed at his own rate through the guide, selecting from among a large number of possible activities and topics which range from the 'simple' to 'complex'. He works largely as an individual, meeting often, however, with a faculty team-member or tutor. Occasionally the whole form is brought together for other, broadly relevant presentations, and group discussion is also used as a teaching technique when appropriate.

As with Kidbrooke, St Dunstan's, and Sevenoaks programs, Kibworth's, too, must be considered tentative and experimental. It was, in my judgment, however, one of the most promising social studies innovations with which I came in contact during my stay in England.

Other developments, both curricular and methodological, might well have been included in the preceding sampling of what appeared to me to be promising new practices. For example (and if space permitted), we might have described at length the stimulating use made of extracts from commercial films such as 'Rebel Without A Cause' in social studies courses developed at Kingsway Day College. We might have described the fascinating projects developed independently and individually by girls at St Paul's School in London during their 'Dalton Week', or the interesting experiments with film-making at Fleetwood School in Surrey, or the many examples of the 'coming of age' of sociology in particular (among the other social sciences) as it is increasingly emphasized in social studies, humanities and general studies syllabuses in England's secondary schools.

Perhaps it would be both appropriate and consistent, however, if we turned away at this time from discussions of experimental syllabuses and new forms of curricular organization in the social studies and explored, instead, some samples of actual classroom practice.

BUSHLOE HIGH SCHOOL

Bushloe is surely one of the most attractive of Leicestershire's 'middle schools'. It is relatively small (about five or six hundred boys and girls) and its energetic Headmaster values the close 'family' relationship he feels can only be obtained in a school of this size. As in Kibworth School, a great deal of attention is paid to the problem of avoiding abrupt and drastic changes from lower school procedures, and to make these transitional years between primary and 'upper' school go as smoothly as possible. Therefore, one teacher will teach a number of subjects to a given first-year class, staying with them for a good part of the school day. By the end of the third year (under the Leicestershire comprehensive plan) students and parents must decide whether or not the children are to go on to the upper school and continue their education or become school leavers at the age of fifteen. Those electing to drop out spend their last year in a unique 'social studies' course. The class (about 75 boys and girls) has as its headquarters a 'temporary' wooden building of its own (called 'Il Ponderosa') located near but quite separate from the main building. Their teacher has the sole responsibility for the education of these soon-to-be school leavers, although he does, of course, solicit the specialized help of other members of the staff from time to time. While the class may study typing, speech, woodwork, etc., the backbone of their program is a broad 'social studies' course. Essentially, the teacher conducts the course by trying to get at questions that are important to his charges—questions that may range all the way from 'who am I and how did I get here?' to, 'What is going on in Africa?' A variety of learning experiences are included, such as visits by the girls to post-natal clinics, visiting lectures by a psychologist on human behavior, etc. During my observations the boys and girls in this class seemed busily and happily occupied. I saw less of the school-leaver discipline problems I observed elsewhere. Other faculty members with whom I spoke felt that the education of these children was being more than adequately handled at Bushloe.

CASTLE ROCK MODERN SECONDARY SCHOOL

Castle Rock is another attractively located school in Leicestershire. It sits near the top of a hill overlooking Coalville—a much prettier town than its name suggests. Only a few hundred yards away is one of England's oldest grammar schools, and, even though some cooperation does exist between the two schools, Castle Rock deals essentially with non-academic children (no subject may be taken to A level there) while the grammar school continues to perform its traditional, university-preparatory function. In this corner of Leicestershire, incidentally, comprehensive secondary education has not as yet become the pattern, even though most of the rest of the area follows the non-selective 'Leicestershire Plan' described briefly earlier.

The Headmaster of this up-to-date, well-equipped, co-educational secondary modern school seemed (as do so many English headmasters and headmistresses) thoroughly involved in the activities, programs, and indeed, in the very lives of his children. He justifiably took pride in the school's magazine and in the achievements of some of his 'outstanding' boys and girls.

Since I had come to Castle Rock to observe the school's social studies course I was taken to the auditorium, where a group of about seventy-five youngsters were meeting under the direction of three teachers. The class was divided into a number of smaller discussion groups, some led by a teacher, others conducted entirely by students. Each group was discussing questions raised earlier. Then (following perhaps ten or fifteen minutes of discussion) a previously designated 'reporter' summarized his or her group's opinions and presented them to the entire class over the public address system. During the year, the class had discussed questions relating to sex, boy-girl relationships, physical appearance, vandalism, the color problem, parent-child conflicts, etc. Prior to the discussion itself, students were asked to think about or respond to questions like these:

The following items were taken from recent newspaper headlines:
1. 19-year-old girl marries man of 40.
2. Boy of 20 marries widow of 45.
3. Chorus girl marries young earl.
4. University student (girl) marries garage mechanic.
5. Negro singer marries British bandleader.
6. Indian doctor marries Irish hospital nurse.

Discuss the type of problems these people are facing. Report on:
1. Say whether your group thinks they are wise or unwise. Give any reasons.
2. What other differences might present problems?
3. What things one should think about in allowing friendships to develop?

A COLOUR PROBLEM

	Yes	No
Which could you do?		
Would you mind sitting next to a coloured pupil?	....	....
Would you mind living next door to a coloured family?	....	....
Would you consider going out for an evening with a coloured boy/girl?	....	....
Would you quite happily accept a coloured girl as your sister-in-law?	....	....

Many people would not like to mix in this way. Why not?
Suggest the three most likely reasons:
A. Fear of their different ways of life.
B. Lack of knowledge about them.
C. Pride in the achievements of white people.
D. Dislike of dark colours, especially black.
E. Worry of what others would say.
F. A feeling that God made white and black and they should therefore stay apart.

PARENTS AND CHILDREN

1. Do parents expect too much from children?
(a) Duties. (b) Behavior. (c) Obedience.
2. Should younger children obey older brothers or sisters and why?
3. Name three sides of growing up which you—as parents— would emphasize with your children.

Discussion was animated in some groups, less so in others. Opinions, as might be expected, were strongly, often emotionally held, and there was little discernible change in opinion. Indeed, the course was conducted largely as a 'non-bookish' discussion course and, apart from the printed, discussion-stimulating questions, no other printed material or other data was distributed.

BACON'S SECONDARY SCHOOL

Bacon's secondary school is located in a poor, near-slum district only a short way from the docks of Southeast London. Its physical plant is obviously ancient, although its precise age is difficult to determine. It has in any event, outside toilets, crumbling plaster here and there, limited play space, rather poor lighting —all the physical defects one might expect to find, since schools do tend to deteriorate with age, despite an occasional face-lifting.

Inside, however, the 'atmosphere' was good. There seemed to be a reasonably wholesome attitude towards school among the rather shabbily dressed (but still in uniform) boys and girls, and the teachers I met seemed alert, friendly and highly professional in their attitudes towards the school and its children.

I went this time to observe a demonstration lesson taught to a group of thirteen and fourteen year olds by a University of London Institute of Education faculty member. A dozen members of his university class had accompanied him, and, indeed, had helped plan the lesson earlier that week. The teacher was concerned with demonstrating to his college class that it *was* possible to teach elements of social science to 'non-academic' children. The lesson itself dealt with clarifying the difference between heredity and environment. The teacher began by reviewing at the blackboard some of the ideas they had discussed and read about previously.

Questions like 'How are people different?' 'What made you (i.e., your "personality") the way you are?' and, 'What *is* intelligence?' were discussed, and, following some obviously confused responses, a series of mimeographed materials was handed out consisting of simple sociological and psychological data dealing with, for example, the raising of identical twins in differing environments, a case history of a girl who had been brought up isolated from society, some material on the breeding of rats, etc. This material was discussed and clarified, and then the class divided into small groups in order to first, make listings of 'things they liked and disliked'—and then, to try to decide whether their reactions were due to heredity or environment. They were to do this, of course, on the basis of insights gleaned from the data they had examined earlier. The lesson lasted well over an hour. The students seemed attentive and interested, and the results of their final, small-group activity indicated a reasonable grasp of the concepts with which the teacher was concerned.

The classroom experiences I have described were, in a sense, all positive. That is, they were taught by well-meaning, well-prepared teachers whose basic objective seemed to be to help children understand the perplexing world in which they live. In all three cases the children were polite, attentive, and co-operative. *The first two*, however (and in marked contrast to the Bacon's school lesson), dramatized some of the problems that those working for reform and improvement in social studies offerings are faced with. To be precise, I found that in the vast majority of schools offering 'social studies' courses (and despite the programs described earlier at Kidbrooke, St Dunstan's, Sevenoaks and Kibworth) social studies was being offered almost exclusively to 'non-academic', 'less-able', 'average or below-average', 'Newsom', 'school-leaving' children. In most cases the quality of such courses was poor—either because the teachers were untrained in the social sciences, or because their conception of what would interest and challenge their students was severely limited by what must now (in the light of recent experience and research) be considered 'conventional wisdom'. To be specific, concern over one's personal appearance is undoubtedly important to an adolescent. But it is not social science. Nor are discussions about vandalism or the color problem social science unless at least some objective data are introduced to create reasonably *informed* opinion—until something approaching the scientific method is used to help one understand *social* phenomena as well as physical phenomena. On the contrary, one might well be accused of conducting *anti* social science programs if one continued simply to divide up into small groups to swap opinions, move from one unrelated question to another, ignore the wealth of data that exists on almost all social problems today, and cater to the lowest common denominators of children's 'interests'.

It is in this context, of course, that the effects of the influential 'Newsom Report' must be evaluated. While the report does give a boost to the social studies idea, the very nature of the document itself, i.e., its specific concern for pupils of 'average and less than average ability' and *its built-in assumption that the education of these children should, of course, be different in kind* from the education of 'above average' children acts as a continuing divisive force in English education.

This may, of course, be largely a matter of interpretation. One *can* find support for a more rigorous, demanding, essentially liberal education in the pages of the Report, *as well* as many references to the importance of the 'practical' aspects of education. In any event, it seems clear (at least to this observer) that the Report is being interpreted by many English educators first, as a demand for more time and attention, more books and equipment for the education of average and below average children. This seems to me to be long overdue in England, and in this sense, Newsom is having a most positive effect. Simultaneously, however, the Report seems to be providing support for those who would continue to provide 'Newsom children' with a type of education that is markedly different from that of the academically able; and this difference is materializing not only in terms of teaching *strategies*, *methods* and *techniques* (an entirely justifiable and reasonable difference, in my opinion), but also in terms of the educational goals and objectives deemed appropriate for both groups of children.

Consider, for example, the three courses of study that follow. Two are brief, while the third is developed in some detail. All are specific responses to the Newsom Report. They are, in my experience, quite representative of social studies courses for 'average and below average' children that are either in the process of development or are currently being taught in English Secondary Schools.

SOCIAL STUDIES COURSE FOR FOURTH YEAR IN A NORTH LONDON SECONDARY SCHOOL

The course was planned to start in September 1964.

PROJECT

The building of a model town ('Newtown') to be sited on the school roof and constructed in hardboard or similar material. This requires section of roof under shed to be enclosed.

AIM

To provide the main focus for a two-year course for *average* and *less able pupils*.

METHOD

(*a*) Newtown to be planned stage by stage in group discussions.
(*b*) Groups to elect mock town councils with officers parallel to those of the adult body.
(*c*) Each instalment of the plan to cover a term's work.
(*d*) Weekly council meetings to be held to discuss progress.
(*e*) All work to be assigned on a weekly or monthly basis depending upon the task allocated.
(*f*) All discussions and reports to be recorded in minute form.

A COURSE IN SOCIAL STUDIES AND CITIZENSHIP FOR FOURTH-YEAR BOYS AND GIRLS IN A SCHOOL IN SUBURBAN LONDON

This course was devised for a group of fourth-year boys and girls in the 14/15 years age range. Its aim was to give some purpose to learning in the last year of their school life and to teach them how to cope with situations they would encounter when they left school.

The course was varied and involved most subject teachers, while one teacher acted as director for the whole course. The varied nature of the course is described below:

(*a*) Writing letters to firms. (Catalogues, requests for information from building societies, requests for details of possible future employment.)

In some cases representatives of the firms contacted subsequently visited the school.

(*b*) Mock interviews between 'employer' and 'applicant', followed by critical discussion.

(c) Mock elections which were preceded by a study of local political parties.
(d) Traffic census followed by construction of graphs and leading to graph-work.
(e) Visits (with definite objectives) to the British Museum, water works, local places of interest. (Local Government visits are also being arranged.)

A TWO-YEAR COURSE IN SOCIAL STUDIES IN A GIRLS' SECONDARY SCHOOL

This course is intended as an alternative to examination courses for girls of average and below average ability. At first, it will be experimental, but it is thought that, ultimately, it will be a two-year course, with an internal certificate awarded to those girls who have satisfactorily taken part in it. A minimum number of textbooks will be used, but, nevertheless, activities will be carefully recorded.

The physical background against which the course is set is very important, so that these new girls, too, can see that their fourth-year work is to open new interests and to have a fresh approach. The rooms which are being provided will, it is hoped, achieve this objective.

Apart from the outline of work which is set out it is hoped that the groups will take part in community service, both inside and outside the school, with particular regard for the needs of the elderly people of the district. Such service should be accepted as a normal part of the adult world which they are setting out to explore.

In addition to the visits mentioned in the course, it is also hoped to organize week-end visits and a group journey, either in this country or abroad.

It is intended that the girls shall be aware of the generous facilities for speakers and visits and that they shall carefully record the way in which money is spent. In addition, the entertainment of speakers and visitors should form an integral part of their social training.

The Youth Employment Officer is also anxious to co-operate and feels that such a course may enable her to get to know the girls fairly well, thus helping her later work.

As well as the work done in their own centre, the groups will take some practical subjects, Physical Education, Speech and Typewriting of French, according to their choice. It is hoped that all this work will be integrated in to the course and that the members of staff teaching groups may meet frequently to discuss problems.

It is hoped to encourage the girls to feel that they can play a real part in maintaining and improving the good 'housing' they have been given, both practically and in raising money to buy extra equipment. In connection with this, it is intended to offer them Club facilities of some sort.

Full use will be made of Sound and Television Broadcasts, the Record Player and Tape Recorder. There will be special interest in recording discussions which follow visits.

Each term the work will fall under two simple, general, headings, 'Myself' and 'Our Homes and the Place where we live'. The following is a temporary plan of work, which may be modified as the facilities of the neighborhood become more apparent through working in them.

TERM I

Myself—Although attention will be given to appearance, it is intended also to emphasize bearing, voice, confidence, reliability and courtesy.

Topics
(1) Care of skin, hair, hands, eyes, teeth, feet. Movement, sensible eating, choice and care of clothes. Grooming.
  Visits—Foot clinic, dental hospital, large shoe store, fabric store, cosmetic factory, eye hospital.
  Possible speakers—Make-up demonstrator, corsetiere, Clarks' speaker and film.
(2) Bearing and voice.
  Possible speakers—from Guildhall and telephone exchange. Telephones on loan from P.O.
(3) Personal spending. Investigation of general teenage spending. The power of advertising.
  Visits—Shop study to survey attack on teenage spending.
(4) Interests.
  Each girl will make a choice from a comprehensive list and present a special study at the end of her course.
(5) My job.
  Visit—from Youth Employment Officer, followed by small and large group discussions. This will be followed next term by further visits and films.

Our homes and the place where we live
(a) Neighborhood study.
The particular neighborhood in which the school is set is very rich in historical and architectural interest and in the lives of those who have lived there in the past. The British Museum, alone, provides opportunities for much interesting work. This project will extend into succeeding terms.
In addition, it is hoped to make a simple study of the workings of local councils.
Visits—Various local visits, including local library work.
Speakers—Architect and local councillor.
(b) How do others live?
Replanning London.
Visits.
(c) Making the most of our homes.
Difficulties and opportunities. Planning, colour, furniture, etc.
Visits—Sandersons, Shand Kydd factory, Heals.

TERM 2
Myself
(a) Bodily Systems—respiratory, circulatory, digestive, reproductive.
Speakers—On smoking, marriage guidance counsellors.
(b) Personal Spending—Income tax, various forms of saving, insurance; N.H. and personal.
Visit—P.O. Savings or other bank.
Speakers—Income tax department; insurance institute (film).
(c) My job—continued from last term.
Visits—to local industries.
Speakers—Personnel officers.

Our homes and the place in which we live
(a) Living in London. Some study of London's history.
Visits—Various in the City.
Westminster and Victoria.
Paddington and Hyde Park.
Exhibitions.
(b) How do others live?
Visits—Suburban area.
Village—special study of village church.

(*c*) Making the most of our homes.
Decorating, curtain making, kitchen planning, repairs, buying a house.
Visits—Design centre, building centre, Ideal Homes Exhibition.
Speaker—From a building society.

TERM 3
Myself
(*a*) Care of a baby. Study of the development of children from birth to five years old. Feeding and clothing children.
Visits—Children's hospital; children's nursery.
Speakers—Mothercraft; Child Care Officer.
(*b*) Personal Spending. Spending in the home. Hire purchase. General utilities.
Visits—Shop investigation into H.P. costs.
Speakers—From Gas, Electricity, and Coal Councils.
(*c*) My job.
Speakers—Panel of girls who have left school.

Living in London
(*a*) London's history and open spaces.
Visits—Hampton, Richmond and Kew.
Hampstead and Kenwood.
Regent's Park and Zoo.
(*b*) How do others live outside London?
Great houses—Hatfield House.
A replanned area—Coventry.
(*c*) Making the most of our homes—electricity; fire, safety in the home.
Speakers—'Do it yourself' expert.
Electrician.
Society for Prevention of Accidents.

These syllabuses obviously speak for themselves. Whatever they are, they bear only the faintest relationship to social science. No self-respecting grammar school staff would consider them anything but 'gut' courses (if I may use an expression coined by American students to describe courses that are unchallenging, unstimulating and obvious). One might ponder seriously whether the social studies courses taught at Kidbrooke,

Kibworth, St Dunstan's and Sevenoaks would not be equally appropriate, equally teachable (although differing teaching techniques may be called for) and, perhaps, ultimately be of far more significance and worth to the children who are currently being exposed to programs similar to those described above.

To turn the argument around for a moment, one also wonders, upon reading sections of some of the better, more *challenging* social studies syllabuses, why such material is often *restricted* to lower streams or 'non-academic' children. Henbury Comprehensive School in Bristol, for example, offers a course for children of 'average and below average ability' which, among other things, includes (at least on paper) the exploration of significant questions concerning the rights and power of trade unions, money as a means of exchange, wealth and society, status and affluence, political decision making, power and conflict, the purpose and nature of education in Britain, etc. These are the sorts of questions that are not generally dealt with in traditional history and geography courses, yet they seem vital matters for *any* citizen to understand and be concerned about—whether he is academic or non-academic, above average or below average, A stream or D stream.

To continue our critical analysis of what seem to me to be weaknesses in English social studies programs, I find myself struck again with the lack of precision, the lack of what might be called a social scientist's perspective or view of the world, indeed, the relative naïvity of many of those writing what are apparently influential books and articles concerning social studies.

Recently, for example, *The Guardian*[1] mentions in its *editorial* column (and quite sympathetically, I must add) a new book dealing with the social studies in schools. The editors felt, apparently, that this area had been too long neglected and they were using this means of giving school social studies a boost. This, then, was the latest thing in print on social studies— and it was reasonably well received among the education public.

To say that the book was a disappointment would be surely a considerable understatement. One gains an inkling of possible

[1] *The Guardian*, 4th March 1966.

problems to follow when one reads, on page 14, that *Arthur Young* wrote *The Rise of Meritocracy*.[1]

In chapter two we read statements like these:

> It is arguable whether Britain's loss of power and prestige in the world is directly connected with a decline in moral standards. Both are generally accepted facts. . . .
>
> Is it not the duty of every teacher to encourage sound social attitudes and higher moral standards? . . .[2]

It is not my purpose here to argue that Britain's prestige in terms of factors other than military power or the periodic problems of the pound has not necessarily declined—that many of us think, for example, that Harold Pinter and Arnold Wesker, among others, may be creating the most provocative plays currently being performed on either side of the Atlantic. Nor shall we debate what 'moral standards' and 'sound social attitudes' are how one measures their decline or ascendency, and whether or not it *is* 'obviously' the duty of every teacher to develop such attitudes and standards. It should be clear, however, that each of these statements is tenuous at best and highly debatable; that the lack of adequate definition of terms results in a situation in which we might argue forever about nothing; and that, in summary, whatever these statements are, they are not social science. We find, therefore, that a further perusal of the book reveals, in the section on 'Planning the Syllabus' that a social studies course should include the following topics, among others:

At Home. A variety of practical courses for boys or girls, often both. For example:

(*a*) Our kitchen. What is essential for a good kitchen? The water supply. How to replace a tap washer. The gas supply. The electric supply. Paying the bills. How to mend a fuse and wire a plug. Heating the home. Safety in the kitchen. Cooking the right food the right way.

(*b*) Handyman. Concreting the garden path. Painting and decorating. Fuses and plugs. Pipes and taps. Toilets and drains. New look for old furniture. Putting up shelves.

---

[1] W. J. Hanson, *Introducing Social Studies*. London: Longman's Green and Co., Ltd, 1966, p. 14.

[2] Ibid., pp. 12, 13.

(*c*) Our Health. A course which will differ for boys and girls. Cleanliness. Personality and appearance. Good clothes. Disease. Preventing accidents. First aid. Problems of adolescence.

Time to Spare? An arts or leisure course covering the life and work of amateur and professional writers, artists, photographers, musicians, actors, and sportsmen.

Looking for a job. The problems of youth employment: security, pay, hours, travel, companionship, training, qualifications, insurance, prospects. Applications and interview.

Getting on with people. At school. The Youth Club. At work. Receiving and entertaining friends. Going steady. Marriage Guidance Council. The Church. Can we secure happiness?

My purpose here is not to pick a particular volume apart. Rather, I feel deeply concerned that this new book has received a relatively uncritical reaction. Surely, if the social studies *are* to have a 'second chance' in England, the approaches outlined in this volume will do little to enhance that possibility, since these ideas are essentially the same as those that floundered so badly in the nineteen fifties.

Indeed, the book is almost a catalogue of practices that have been roundly criticized and rejected elsewhere—yet continue to find favor among the majority of 'social studies' supporters here. For example, the results and insights of recent research in the social sciences and in education are seldom utilized, and we find essentially unsupportable statements like these continuing to appear:

> I believe the best foundation for a social studies scheme beginning in the third year of the secondary school is a course of *Local Studies in the preceeding two years when interest in the natural and physical environment may be at its height.*[1] [Italics mine.]

Illustrations of the sort of learning activity implied in the above statement appear somewhat later in the book:

> Make a quick sketch of the church on your second sheet of paper.

---

[1] Ibid., p. 7.

Of what materials are the walls built?
What material was used for the roof?
About how high is the tower?
When you enter the church, look first at the diagram hanging on the first pillar and then answer these questions:
At what period and date was the doorway built?
Which is the oldest part of the church?
Which part of the church is the nave?
Which part of the church is the aisle?
After whom is the chapel named?
Why was the chapel so planned?

Draw a plan of the church on your third sheet of paper.

Turning left from the door, walk down the aisle and look at the wall opposite the fifth pillar. What do you see?

What scene is depicted in the stained glass window above the altar?
Which of the windows do you like best?

Look at the organ. When was it built? Where did the money come from to buy it?

Go to the porch and look for the following information:
When are services held on Sunday?
How was the money from last month's collection used?

What activities are run during the week by the Church?

Why was the Church built?[1]

We have dealt with the obsession some educators have for the local or parochial elsewhere in our discussion of the teaching of history and geography. It is enough to say here that the same unquestioned acceptance of this sometimes overwhelming attention to the nearby seems to go beyond the bounds of reason.

Jerome Bruner's comments concerning localism might well be worth the most careful consideration by English educators working to develop more effective social studies curricula:

[1] Ibid., p. 49.

. . . a point of view quite different from ours . . . holds that one should begin teaching social studies by presenting the familiar world of home, the street, and the neighborhood. It is a thoroughly commendable ideal; its only fault is its failure to recognize how difficult it is for human beings to see generality in what has become familiar. The 'friendly postman' is indeed the vicar of federal powers, but to lead the child to the recognition of such powers requires many detours into the realm of what constitutes power, federal or otherwise, and how, for example, constituted power and willfully exercised force differ. We would rather find a way of stirring the curiosity of our children with particulars whose intrinsic drama and human significance are plain— whether close at hand or at a far remove. If we can evoke a feeling for bringing order into what has been studied, the task is well started.[1]

Similarly, one finds that social studies courses (as with history and geography) often tend to be emasculated in their treatment of conflict in modern life—even though they often purport to be far more 'relevant' than 'traditional' courses. Local studies and surveys tend to catalogue, not evaluate; historical studies seldom deal with conflicting, competing ideas; units or topics on home or family (for example) fail to examine the family as a *universal* phenomenon with both comforting similarities to our own way of life as well as fascinating, but *explainable* and *reasonable* differences. And again, the real problems faced by families living in an urban, mobile, rapidly changing society are seldom investigated (if they are investigated at all) in anything approaching the objective, data seeking, reasoned approach of the social scientist.

Undoubtedly further criticisms might be made, other questions raised. However, the more I visited schools in England, examined syllabuses and textbooks, and talked with school, college, and university teachers, the more convinced I became that many of the curricular 'weaknesses' that troubled me were attributable perhaps, to rather differing perceptions here and in the United States concerning the task of curriculum development. (Other 'weaknesses', of course, are attributable to my

[1] Jerome Bruner, *Man: A Course of Study*. Occasional Paper No. 3, The Social Studies Curriculum Program, Educational Services, Inc., Cambridge, Mass., June 1965, p. 20.

own biases, attitudes, and experiences which, unfortunately, I was unable to leave behind.) That is, the development of a new social studies curriculum takes time—and lots of it. It is exceedingly difficult to carry out a task as complex as this in after-school hours or on weekends. Similarly, money is needed—not only to free competent people to spend large blocks of time on the problem, but also to bring in professional, secretarial, and other help when necessary. Given these conditions, it then becomes at least *possible* to take a long, hard look at what one has been doing—at what current research tells us—at what others are doing—at where *we* want to go. Like God, Motherhood and Democracy, everyone is in favor of teaching children to think. But what precisely do we mean by thinking? What, specifically, are the skills we hope to teach children? At what age level should a given skill be introduced? How often and when should it be reinforced? What are the attitudes and values that we want to develop in children? Do they mean the same thing to everyone, or are they really rather nebulous statements? If so, how can we make them more precise? What kinds of learning experiences are most likely to bring about the behavioral and intellectual changes implied in our curriculum? How do we evaluate whether or not we have been successful?

Obviously, these are *not* easy questions to answer. Yet, if we are to avoid constructing 'scissors and paste' re-hashes of what has gone before, they must be answered.

Perhaps one of the most promising attempts to outline what ought to be included in a secondary school social studies course (and surely one that comes very close indeed to meeting many of the criticisms raised in this chapter) is the Nuffield Foundation's working paper dealing with a hypothetical course of study for fourteen- to sixteen-year-olds called 'Man in Society'.[1] It is, of course, in an exceedingly tentative form at present, and the syllabus that ultimately emerges may bear little resemblance to what appears below. Nevertheless, even a cursory examination of it ought to reveal its close relationship to the social sciences, the broad scope of its topics, and the respect it seems to imply for the abilities, interests, and maturity of the students who may use it.

[1] This course was published in a modified form as the Schools Council Working Paper No. 11.

I. *The Nature of Man*

   (*a*) *Elementary human biology* (some sex instruction, and some facts about race differences and their relative biological insignificance could be included).

   (*b*) *Elementary psychology* (something about unconscious drives; inheritance and environment; the abilities and limitations of the human brain; the relation of psychology and physiology).

   (*c*) Developing out of (*a*) and (*b*), *human relationships*: social, occupational, and sexual (some social psychology could come in here—the pressures of conformity and of advertising and propaganda; the action of rumour and prejudice; the psychology of groups).

   (*d*) Developing out of (*c*), some consideration of *attitudes and values* (morality and literature): one might here encourage careful and systematic discussion of the pupils' own problems—adolescent worries, parent-child conflict —bringing in psychological facts and social examples from other societies.

   (*e*) Developing out of (*d*), *visions and ideals* (religion and the arts): one might discuss some movements and individuals that look beyond the easily seen world. Are they right? or wrong, but important? Or useless? Do they help or hinder our understanding of 'Man in Society'?

II. *The Nature of Human Society*

   (*a*) *Our own society* (the idea of looking at what goes on socially as something first to be checked factually, then analyzed objectively—the difference between fact and judgment).

   (*b*) *Other societies, past and present* (some indication of the enormous range of social systems—including those of local immigrants—the existence, for example, of types of family very unlike our own, but not therefore 'inferior').

   (*c*) Developing out of (*a*) and (*b*), the *relationship between society and its environment* (including perhaps a close study of the local area and two or three very different areas).

   (*d*) Developing out of (*a*), (*b*) and (*c*) some very elementary *social and economic ideas* (systematic connections between social events; production of goods and services—the division of labour between occupations and between areas; personal incomes—how what is produced is consumed).

(*e*) Also developing out of (*a*), (*b*) and (*c*), *the evolution of society* (pastoral, agricultural, urban) and *aspects of economic growth* (e.g. the history of British industry from the industrial revolution; the important role of investment and savings).

(*f*) Developing out of (*d*) and (*e*), a study of *a particular social system in action* (e.g. school, factory, gang or club).

(*g*) Also developing out of (*d*) and (*e*), some study of *civics and politics* (involving outside visits and outside visitors as well as books): (i) British institutions—the roles of local and central government (what is the 'council' and how does it affect me?); the nature and financing of public services (health, education, transport, housing); the law and the trade unions; (ii) the British political system—parliament and the franchise; the main political parties; (iii) other political systems (e.g. the U.S.A., Russia).

III. (Following on from I and II) *The Issues of Modern Society.* A choice of one of two of the following options for detailed study (depending both on the particular interests of pupils and on the particular specialisms of teachers):

(*a*) The achievements of technology: the ubiquity of mathematics and statistics; the use of computers; automated production; the implications for retraining and the use of leisure.

(*b*) *International relations:* the conflicts of Eastern and Western ideologies; war and peace (the two world wars; the nuclear deterrent and the balance of power; the role of the United Nations); anti-colonialism and the world colour issue; international trade.

(*c*) *The gap between nations:* the developing countries of Africa and Asia; problems of immigration; world-over-population; hunger and disease; international aid.

At this writing a number of promising projects appear to have been stimulated by some of the ideas that appeared in the Nuffield paper described above. For example, the Schools Council has joined with the Nuffield Foundation in support of a 'Humanities Curriculum Project'. Intended for fourteen- to sixteen-year-olds, the project will attempt to make available to interested teachers inquiry-based, interdisciplinary teaching materials—materials dealing with topics drawn from history, geography, religion, and the social sciences. The Nuffield-Schools Council Group will *not* produce a syllabus: rather it will attempt to give stimulus and support to teachers through the creation of illustrative materials. At the moment, materials dealing with themes, such as urbanization, war and peace, law and order, the family, and relations between the sexes are being prepared. The project team is gathering tapes, news items, data from interviews, reproductions of paintings, photographs, etc., as the 'raw material' for learning and expects to try out some of their materials experimentally in 1968.

Similarly, Nuffield is working on another collaborative venture—this one with the Goldsmith's College Curriculum Laboratory. This group is attempting to develop a first-year secondary school course emphasing 'interdisciplinary enquiry' in the humanities.

Some schools are not waiting for Nuffield or the Schools Council and are simply ploughing ahead on their own. One of the most promising of these is the five-year course currently being developed at Cressex School in Buckinghamshire. Its emphasis is on Social Science—its concepts, data and methods —taught within a context of socio-cultural significance.

It is in this direction that social studies needs to go, I think, if it is to avoid the fate that overtook it two decades ago.

VI: OTHER FACTORS CONTRIBUTING TO THE SOCIAL EDUCATION OF ENGLISH SECONDARY SCHOOL CHILDREN

A RECENTLY PUBLISHED study of Winchester College includes the following description of the peculiar mark or sign of a boy from Winchester:

> We put the emphasis on intellect and we try and set a very high standard. A Winchester boy is likely to be capable of hard work and devotion to duty, which are valuable in almost all careers. Philosophy, politics and literary judgment come in more and more at the top of the school.
>
> Reliability is achieved, and often originality. But the Wykehamist isn't an extremist. He isn't allowed to display naïve enthusiasm. That may be something to do with our mugging-hall system: the boys having cubicles to work in, and not studies as a rule. I'm anxious to build a new House with studies, and add study blocks to the others. It would be interesting to see if there was a change in the sort of boys we turn out.
>
> One thing which is common to pretty well all Wykehamists is the ruthless reduction of things to size, which means that enthusiasms are always questioned. Nobody and nothing is to be admired, at least uncritically, including the Headmaster. Boasting, or putting on an act, is dealt with quite brutally. Boys have a vivid turn of expression, which can be devastating.[1]

One might compare it with these excerpts from the Bedales Prospectus:

> Coeducation . . . involves not merely the joint education of boys and girls under teachers of both sexes, but also the sharing, to the fullest possible extent, in most of the ordinary activities of school life. Most school occupations are all the better for being shared by boys and girls.

---

[1] C. Dilke, *Dr. Moberly's Mint-Mark: A Study of Winchester College*. London: William Heinemann, 1965, p. 175.

While boys and girls at Bedales are trusted with rather more liberty than is usual at most schools, they are encouraged to feel that they are themselves responsible for the right use of it, and the elder also for the younger. As large a share as possible in the management of the school life is given to the older boys and girls; and the younger also have definite duties assigned to them, in order to give them opportunities of being of service to the community.

Although careful attention is paid to the needs of the individual child, co-operation rather than competition is emphasized as a motive to action. Marks are seldom used, and there are no form-orders or prizes. We hold that a high standard of achievement for the sake of the work itself, and the feeling of co-operation in something that is shared by all, are better incentives than hope of reward or fear of punishment.[1]

Quite obviously, Winchester and Bedales differ a good deal in terms of the product they are aiming to produce. Both schools would agree, however, that whatever their goals and objectives, only limited progress towards achieving them can be made within the bounds of conventional courses. The entire school program—curricular and extra-curricular—is designed with a given school's goals in mind, and we must examine something more than history, geography, or social studies syllabuses in order to gain a complete picture of the social education of children in a given school.

English

Islington Green Secondary School is neither a Bedales nor a Winchester. On the contrary, it is what Americans euphemistically refer to as an 'inner city' school which caters to 'culturally disadvantaged' children. Nevertheless, I observed an English lesson there that, in my judgment, can fairly be described as superb. Simply stated, the class consisted of fourteen- and fifteen-year-old 'non-academic' girls who were studying Arnold Wesker's play, *Roots*, in their English class. Their teacher had his charges discussing at a mature, intelligent level, the structure of a given scene; for example, how it built

[1] *Bedales School Prospectus*. Petersfield, Hampshire. January 1966, pp. 2, 3.

to a pitch, then dropped. Two of the girls gave particularly sensitive readings to excerpts from the play, and then the teacher encouraged them to discuss its implications for *their* lives. While they did not use the language of sociology, they animatedly discussed for over thirty minutes problems related to the conflict between generations, values, class, and education.

Many teachers of English seem to accept the notion that one does not have to learn the mother tongue in a sterile, idea-less vacuum. Therefore, textbooks often include selections designed to awaken social awareness in their readers. For example, perceptive English teachers have developed courses or units of study around themes such as 'The Limitations of Censorship', in which sixth formers are asked to read books like Francois Mauriac's *God and Mammon*, Jacques Maritain's *Art and Poetry*, and Matthew Arnold's *Culture and Anarchy*. Reading lists in courses on 'The Adolescent' include Margaret Mead's *Coming of Age in Samoa* as well as Kingsley Amis' *Lucky Jim* and John Osborne's *Look Back in Anger*. Courses in 'American Life and Literature' encourage English adolescents to read a number of books that are becoming increasingly difficult to use in American high schools because of their alleged 'obscenity'; for example, J. D. Salinger's *Catcher in the Rye*, Joseph Heller's *Catch—22*, Vladimir Nabokov's *Lolita* and James Baldwin's *Another Country*.

Religious Education

At its best (and admittedly, this is rare) a course in Religious Education can also make significant contributions to a child's understanding of his complex, diverse, and challenging world. One cannot ignore the probable impact of the type of lesson I observed in a girls' grammar school during a class centered upon a discussion of the Virgin birth. The teacher—a highly intelligent, mature woman who surely deserves to be called a master teacher—attempted to handle this ultimately as an example of the Christian conception of the relationship of Jesus to God, of the 'logic' behind Christianity. This led to a brief discussion of the assumptions of Buddhism and Hinduism (which they had already studied) and to the tentative conclusion that each made sense in terms of its assumptions. At no point in the lesson did she attempt to 'sell' Christianity as such, and she was scrupulously objective (yet marvelously stimulating) in her handling of the beliefs of others.

While it would be impossible to say that courses in religious education generally followed this pattern, it would be equally difficult to conclude that 'R.I.' makes no contribution to one's knowledge and understanding of the world and its people. I saw similarly effective discussions at other schools—particularly in those where time had been taken to develop specific units or topics in comparative religion. If one can assume that the study of the religious (and non-religious) beliefs and values of others is becoming a more acceptable facet of religious education here, one can expect 'R.I.' to make increasing contributions to a child's broad social education. It seems to me, incidentally, that studies of comparative religion, religious history and conflict, the religious beliefs of selected non-literate or simple societies, the beliefs and arguments of agnostics, atheists, humanists, and others, offer English educators a rare opportunity to make a challenging, worthwhile and meaningful contribution to the education of secondary school children.

I think it is fair to say that Religious Education in England is finding it increasingly difficult to justify its curricular existence—apart from the fact that it is mandated by law. Without attempting a cataloguing of its weaknesses (something many English educators have done far more effectively and at much greater length than would be possible here[1]), it appears to be relatively ineffective in terms of achieving its avowed purposes. As Harold Loukes put it, the British people like having religion around 'for coronations, weddings and funerals'.[2] Apart from these functions, they are not at all sure of its value, significance, or importance in their lives. Given this situation, one would hope that those responsible for this segment of the curriculum might seriously consider the adoption of far more objective, intellectually demanding and less doctrinaire studies *about* religion rather than *in* religion.

[1] See, for example, the writings of Harold Loukes, Reader in Education at Oxford University and Dr Ronald J. Goldman.

[2] H. Loukes, 'Honest To Children', *Where*, Winter, 1965, No. 19, p. 8.

Social Service and other activities

> We go on Social Service to help other people who are old and can't get about. I think it a good idea, because as well as helping them, it gives us a sense of responsibility. It also makes a change from ordinary lessons. The lady I visit doesn't even have a Home Help, and when we go, we do all that seems necessary, cleaning, scrubbing, and tidying up. When we have finished, we make a cup of tea, and sit and talk to her. I don't think we have enough time there, because if she wants to go for a walk, we haven't time to take her and to do the work as well. She doesn't know what she'd do without us.

American students of English education are usually impressed with the many ways in which English secondary school children are expected to provide various forms of local service for those who cannot help themselves. Indeed, I sometimes think that Britain's elderly—those whom Americans refer to as having reached the 'golden age'—must be among the most pampered in the world! School after school has arranged programs involving visits similar to that described above.

Quite obviously, these experiences can and often do help young people to understand better the realities of the world in which they live, the problems faced by many citizens, as well as the role and responsibility of government in alleviating such problems. Similarly, one might expect that young people so involved would develop more positive, sympathetic attitudes towards the aged. It seemed to me, however, that many service programs tended to ignore the fact that geriatrics (for example) is, after all, a very complicated subject. Students were sent out with little in the way of background information or understanding. Again, data from the appropriate social (and other) sciences was sparingly used, and one wonders if some students may come away from such experiences not with a better understanding of the behavior of the elderly but rather, with feelings of revulsion concerning old-age.

In other words, while the essential purposes of such programs seem sound, care *does* need to be taken that some real understanding results from them; that participants are carefully selected, that ample time is allowed for supportive, clarifying study and discussion, and that children come away from such experiences with increasing insight about the 'why's' of human behavior. This does not, in my experience, happen automatically.

Perhaps this description of the Sevenoaks Voluntary Service Unit may provide a positive illustration of a school service program that anticipated many of the problems outlined above and appears, therefore, to be one that might well serve as a model for others:

> The social service effort at Sevenoaks is by no means unique; but it is distinguished from the general run of schemes by its scale and by the care with which it is planned. Started five years ago, the unit now has over a hundred girls and a hundred boys drawn from five schools in the area. The range of work undertaken includes help to elderly people in their homes and in a geriatric ward, work with children in an approved school and in a school for the blind, the manning of road crossings and re-afforestation. Membership of the unit is voluntary; indeed the headmaster went to some lengths at the outset to discourage volunteers, in order that the scheme should be built up slowly. In the ordinary way those who join the unit must commit themselves for one or two hours a week throughout a term. For some jobs a longer term commitment is required; two boys learning braille in order to give backward readers some extra help have agreed to stay with the job for at least two years.
>
> The jobs are found and cleared with the voluntary and statutory authorities by adults. To ensure continuity, some of the young people continue with the work during holiday time. Of 350 boys in the school over 15, more than a hundred are now regularly involved in the voluntary service unit.[1]

English children learn about their world in dozens of other ways as well. Local and foreign travel, including 'study cruises' to places as far away as Stockholm, Helsinki, and Leningrad are becoming increasingly popular, as are foreign exchange visits with students in France, Holland, and other European countries. For example, one might examine De Burgh Comprehensive School's listing of local and foreign visits in 1964–65 to get some idea of the range of out-of-school 'social study' that is possible at many schools:

---

[1] *New Society*, 23rd October 1965, p. 13.

School Visits—1964–65

Geological Museum (2).

Field work at Reigate Hall.

Dale Fort Field Study Centre. Pembrokeshire.

Rambles to Leith Hill and St Leonards Forest.

Youth hostelling at Brighton, Hastings, and Holmbury.

The Tate Gallery (3).

Epsom Art School.

Snowdonia.

Electrical Research Association.

Sutton Waterworks.

Trampolining Finals at Royal Albert Hall (2).

International Gymnastic Finals: U.S.A. and Great Britain at Wembley.

Sundry Theatres.

Rock climbing, North Wales.

Victoria and Albert Museum.

Express Dairy Milk Bottling Plant.

Henley Fort Camp (1 week).

British Museum.

P O. Sorting Office (Epsom).

Epsom Fire Station.

Borough of Sutton.

Festival Hall.

St Mary's Church, Burgh Heath.

Banstead Hospital Chapel.

Commonwealth Institute (9).

Mole Valley, Burgh Heath

National History Museum.

Wildenstein's Art Gallery.

Sutton Art School.

Royal Institution.

Olympic Gymnastics.

A (T.V.) studio.

Crystal Palace Sports Centre.

Ideal Home Exhibition.

Nature Trails.

London Museum.

Crawley New Town.

Surrey Fire Brigade H.Q.

Banstead U.D.C.

Surrey County Council.

Fairfield Halls.

Foreign Visits, 1964–65

Spain, Austria, France, Switzerland.

Similarly, current events 'clubs', BBC programs such as 'Talks for Sixth Forms', and the encouragement of informal study groups also make their contributions. (I vividly recall the hand-written notice on a bulletin board at Dartington Hall requesting that 'anyone interested in studying comparative religion this term please sign below'. Nine names were on the list, and I must confess to a degree of envy at this, and other similar opportunities, offered students at schools like Dartington.) One cannot help but be impressed also with Sevenoaks 'International House', in which about twenty-five sixth formers from all over the world live and study together.

Student government also makes its contribution to social

understanding in schools where young people are given the kind of responsibility that removes them from the 'paper parliament' category so typical of student government both here and in the United States. At Rosebery Grammar School, for example, student government was a *reality*. I attended a meeting of the school council in their own (suitably messy) prefect room—a meeting in which a mature, intelligent group of sixteen- to eighteen-year-old girls met to both discuss and *act upon* a variety of school problems. (The girls, incidentally, wore 'street clothes', rather than school uniforms, following a recent *council* action.)

General Studies

Perhaps the most influential 'peripheral' contributors to English students' understanding of topics, concepts, ideas, and events that might ordinarily be included in the domain of geography, history, or social studies are the 'general studies' offered in the sixth forms of most schools.

It is common knowledge that those responsible for the selection of students for university places value outstanding performance in a secondary school student's A level examinations above all else when considering him for admission to a university. The student is seen, of course, as a potential historian, mathematician or physicist, and how well he performs in his area of specialization will determine more than any other factor whether or not he will win a coveted university place. This means, of course, that specialization begins early in secondary schools, and that students are likely to enter the sixth form with a number of glaring gaps in their general education. Whether or not this is a 'good' or a 'bad' thing is, of course, highly debatable, and English educators seem to be involved in a continuing discussion of specialization's pros and cons. Nevertheless, those who feel that university entrance ought to be decided on something more than A level passes in a few specialized subjects have at least brought about some 'paper commitments' from university officials to the effect that general education, too, is important. Whether anything but A level performance *is* actually considered in the decision-making process in most universities is hard to fathom; nevertheless, there is considerable pressure to alter the balance between general and special studies in the sixth form.

In any event 'general studies' (sparked by the dynamic and increasingly influential General Studies Association) has become more and more common, and such programs were offered in virtually every sixth form I visited.

The programs or syllabuses themselves, of course, vary considerably. Ideally, they would draw more or less equally upon the insights of 'Science, Society, Philosophy, and the Arts', as R. Irvine Smith put it. Since we are particularly concerned with the nature of the 'society' component, however, it would seem appropriate at this point to examine that aspect of general studies.

To begin with, one might find virtually any topic offered under the social studies or 'societal' heading in general studies courses. I found, for example, courses in 'American Studies', 'Fifth-Century Athens', an 'Introduction to Economics', 'Civics', 'The Soviet Union', 'Britain Today', 'The Cold War', and 'The Influence of Freud on Modern Society', among many others.

Rather than dwell on the scope of general studies, however, let us examine at least one program in some depth.

Rosebery Grammar School—an institution that has already been referred to a number of times in this study—has probably had more success with its general studies program than any other school I know of in England. It surely stood head and shoulders above similar programs I encountered in the schools I visited. Rosebery has developed a general studies course that is one of the school's primary attractions. The course was conceived not as a dangling appendage to the traditional A level subjects generally taken in the sixth form, but rather as a general education core out of which specialized studies might grow. A great deal of the headmistress's and her staff's time went into the planning of general studies at Rosebery, and the immediate result of these efforts was the most unusual situation in which practically *all* of the girls undertake sixth-form work rather than leave after the completion of G.C.E. O level examinations. Many girls who might ordinarily leave stayed on because of the broad appeal of the sixth form, and Rosebery is now faced with a situation in which numbers of students from neighboring schools are clamoring to transfer into Rosebery's sixth form and participate in its general studies course.

The Rosebery program consists of required courses in philosophy, religion, current events, English, and either art or music. In addition, girls may take political philosophy, classical background, general mathematics, general science and logic—depending upon their interests. (University candidates, however, are expected to take the *entire* series.) While a printed syllabus cannot effectively communicate the overall excellence of the Rosebery program, the following relevant excerpts should give the reader some idea of the role general studies plays in providing education about man and society *outside* the framework of courses in history, geography or social studies.

PHILOSOPHY

IN THE FIRST YEAR SIXTH

I. *General Introduction to theory of knowledge*
   (a) Discussion of empirical knowledge as contrasted with intuitive knowledge (knowledge of values).
   (b) Limitations of empirical knowledge.
   (c) Difficulties of intuitive knowledge—discussion of meaning of absolute and relative values.
   (d) Contrast of two different theories of values, Christian and Greek, and two ways of life, Christianity and humanism, with a digression of the influence of social environment.

II. For the rest of the year empirical knowledge and the scientific method with special consideration of:
   (a) Dangers in use of language.
   (b) Dangers arising from prejudice.
   (c) Dangers in use of inductive method.
       Observation and generalization.
   (d) Dangers in use of deduction.

POLITICAL PHILOSOPHY

AIM

To give an introduction in very broad outline to the main political theorists and their theories, showing how new ideas about the organization of society arise out of contemporary circumstances.

Discussion and comparison with modern thought and practice should naturally arise from the lessons, and the last term is devoted to discussion of general essay questions.

No homework is set or specific reading demanded. Cross references to R.I., classical background, etc.

Greek City State. Plato and Aristotle.

Later Greek theories such as Epicureanism and Stoicism.

Organization of Roman Empire. Roman Law.

Conflict between Christianity and Roman ideas.

Medieval theories. St Augustine. Feudalism.

Rise of absolute monarchies. Machiavelli and absolute theory.

Protestant theories. Luther. Calvin.

Beginning of democratic theory. Hobbes. Locke.

French revolutionary theory. Montesquieu, Voltaire, Rousseau. Utilitarianism.

Liberalism of John Stuart Mill.

Marxism. Communism in Russia. Socialism in England. Fascism. Nineteenth-century imperialism.

Theories of modern political parties in England.

Rise of modern nationalism. Internationalism. League of Nations and United Nations.

CURRENT EVENTS

No set syllabus; literally current events in widest possible sense. Subjects often suggested by girls and lessons often conducted by them. Anything topical discussed and explained.

Knowledge of current events also increased by membership of Council for Education in World Citizenship (voluntary for members of sixth forms). Outside lecturers invited, debates and discussions held and expeditions to places such as *The Times* Offices, Stock Exchange, Lloyds, Parliament and Law Courts arranged.

During the two years part of the current events courses will be taken over by the economics master. The following subjects will be studied:

1. Meaning and scope.
2. The pricing system—perfect competition and monopoly.
3. Labour and wages.
4. The national income.
5. The national income and international trade (balance of payments).

It would be entirely unfair and inadequate, however, to conclude this treatment of general studies on a completely positive note. As I visited school after school, talked to students and staff members, and examined literally dozens of syllabuses, a number of weaknesses persistently appeared.

To begin with, even at Rosebery there was seldom enough time to handle all of the topics adequately. At other schools that were not, perhaps, as committed to the general studies idea, the time problem was worse.

At one school, for example, I sat through a fascinating presentation by a rather mystical young man concerning 'the existence of God'. His case was exceedingly well presented and well argued. It included reference to research by men like Rhine on extra-sensory perception, and ended with a poignant plea for his cynical young audience not to reject his case out of hand—that two thousand years of Christianity is too much to casually throw away. He presumed he would reject some of his own arguments as he grew and matured and as new evidence appeared, and he hoped that he and his classmates would attempt to evaluate his position logically, scientifically, and without prejudice or bias.

Obviously, this young man had spent hours preparing his presentation. He refused to be bound by what he considered to be inadequate time limits, either in or out of class. His report was superb.

This study was followed by two other presentations. One of these was a ten-minute treatment of the 'New Africa'. In contrast to the first presentation, this one was sketchy, undocumented, and shallow; further, it was considerably more representative of the sort of activity I observed in general studies classes than was the report on 'The existence of God'.

If it is possible to generalize, one might say that there is far too much of this sort of superficiality in the treatment of quite complex social science-related topics. In schools where it would be considered standard procedure to take, perhaps, ten days to study and pick apart a novel like *A Passage to India*, topics such as 'the changing family' are handled in an afternoon's discussion.

Part of this problem is undoubtedly related to the tendency in some schools to select one or two of the school's more 'offbeat' faculty members to teach general studies, usually with the Head's admonition to go ahead and 'stimulate' them (i.e., the students), in any way that seems reasonable. Thus general studies can become a laissez faire repository for staff-room characters and clowns who are now (unhappily, from the students' point of view) provided with a captive audience.

In any event, in many of the schools I visited, general studies was not taken terribly seriously. As one might expect, the typical student reaction was something like, 'I enjoy classroom discussion, but I really can't give any time to general studies outside of class because of A level pressures.' This reaction (and one must remember that, while in my opinion it *predominates*, it is *not* universal), is due, of course, as much to general studies' importance (or lack of it) in the eyes of those in charge of university admission as to any other factor. While both A and O level examinations in General Studies exist (and indeed, in Northern England are taken by large numbers of students) most universities refuse to take them seriously as evidence for admission or rejection, and students therefore react accordingly.

None of this should be taken as a lack of interest in the fundamental idea of general studies on the part of the students. I was constantly struck with the apparently sincere interest expressed by many of the youngsters I interviewed in a broader, more liberal, less specialized education. However, they, too, recognize that they are part of 'the system'—and until 'the system' is changed, student priorities will probably continue to go where an academic 'pay off' seems most likely.

VII: EXAMINATIONS AND THE SOCIAL STUDIES

THE SATIRIC, iconoclastic British television program 'B.B.C. 3' began each week with a song about the persistence and essential sameness of man's achievements, follies and blunders. It was called simply, 'Its All Been Done Before'.

So much has been 'done before' on the subject of examinations in England that there is probably little that I can write that has not already been said or written; and the chances are that it has been expressed more effectively and thoroughly than what appears below.

Nevertheless, examinations are so much a part of English education that they deserve some special place in a study of this kind, and perhaps the fact that I can at least view them with the perspective of an outsider may justify the inclusion of this chapter.

We should begin, perhaps, by underscoring the ubiquitousness and significance of national examinations in English life. The G.C.E. is indeed a passport to the better managerial and professional careers, and entrance to college or university depends almost entirely upon G.C.E. passes.

Similarly, the continued (although declining) existence of the 'eleven plus' examination puts tremendous pressure on many young children to leap the main hurdle that obstructs their way to a grammar school (or grammar 'stream') education. Even those whose interests do not lie in managerial or professional directions still find themselves caught in the examination tide, taking, perhaps, the new C.S.E. which is geared to 'average students . . . for whom the G.C.E. is not an entirely suitable examination'.[1]

Given the significance of examinations in England, then, let us attempt to look more closely at G.C.E. papers in history and geography in particular, the C.S.E. papers in history geography and social studies, and the eleven-plus examination. My essential concern, incidentally, will be with the papers as *examinations*

[1] *C.S.E.* Southeast Regional Examination Board, Tunbridge Wells, Kent.

rather than as courses of study, since curricular problems have been treated in general elsewhere. Nevertheless, some comments relating to what seem to be significant omissions, over-emphases, etc., will undoubtedly appear.

The G.C.E. in History

The reader will recall that O level history tends to place most of its emphasis upon *British* and *European* history, *prior* to 1940. (The London Board's course in world affairs from 1919 to the present must still be considered experimental, and it has yet to gain wide acceptance in the schools. The same can be said for the latest syllabuses developed by the Joint Matriculation Board and the Associated Examining Board.)

Regardless of which Examining Board syllabus one chooses, or the particular topics or periods studied by a given class or form, however, history examination questions at O level tend to a frightening sameness. Consider, for example, the following quite representative questions:

> Give an account of the achievements of Alfred in war and peace.
> Why did Frederick Barbarossa quarrel with the Papacy and what was the outcome of this?
> What English settlements were made during the reigns of James I and Charles I either in North America or in the West Indies?
> What were England's chief imports in the fourteenth and fifteenth centuries?

Similarly, the 'outline' questions that appear on many examination papers, e.g., 'outline British policy towards Ireland between 1801 and 1846' would appear to fall into the same basic category.

I think it would be quite fair to say that the vast majority of O level questions fit this classification, i.e., they are questions emphasizing either a pupil's *memory* abilities, or, what Guilford, Taylor, Getzels, Torrance and others call *convergent* thinking—thinking which leads to one, right, recognized best, and conventional answer. Cognitive abilities—those used in recognition, discovery, understanding or comprehension are seldom tested. Nor is there evidence of concern for *divergent* thinking which leads to the exploration of *many* possible solutions to a given problem, or evaluative abilities used in determining the adequacy of ideas or information produced through either convergent or divergent thinking.

In other words, if one ignores the factual make-up of history O level questions, one finds that the examiners are, essentially, testing the same sorts of mental abilities over and over again.

If, of course, one is committed to the position that pre-sixth form pupils are expected largely to *memorize*, while those reaching the magic, inner sixth form circle are expected to *think*, the questions listed above are as adequate as any to test the success or failures of one's program. That is, the approach taken by the nine G.C.E. examining boards is 'wrong' only if one holds a differing set of objectives for pre-sixth form history teaching. Clearly, most American educators *would* disagree heartily with this position, and this disagreement is reflected, I think, in both the nature of many of the newer teaching materials found in American secondary (and elementary) schools, as well as in the diversity of the evaluative devices utilized in school and classroom testing programs.

One might object also to questions that, while they may not call for a given 'right' answer, are so broad—so vague—that it would take the combined talents of a half a dozen historians adequately to answer them, if indeed, adequate answers are possible, for example: 'Consider the merits and defects of F.D.R. as leader of the U.S. in peace and war.' or, 'Why did Germany lose the Second World War?'

Other problems appear as well—although they may be attributable more to the structure of the syllabus than to the inadequacies of the examination. One cannot help but notice, for example, the rarity of questions calling for some sort of *social* (in contrast to political) understanding of historical problems. To illustrate, a question on American history asks, 'What attempts were made to settle the dispute over slavery before 1861?' One can visualize a student dutifully reproducing the list of 'attempts' appearing in his notebook—all the while having little or no conception of what it means to have been a slave in the American South during this period. Questions seeking to assess a student's understanding of the pattern of life to which a slave was subjected—*his* (i.e. the slave's) perceptions and the perceptions of whites concerning slavery as an institution—these seldom appear.

Occasionally, questions such as 'What were the main social and economic problems of the Tudors?' were asked. These obviously called for non-political responses. They were rare, however, and when they did appear they often lacked the focus that would demand something more than superficial understanding.

Neither was there any considerable attempt to link the past with the present—to test one's ability to relate concepts like 'serfdom' or 'slavery' to current problems. On the contrary, anything current (as might be expected) received minimal attention. One examination dealing with European history from the reign of Constantine until World War II included only two questions out of thirty-six on events following World War I.

Other problems concerned me as well; for example, the tendency to allow so many options (students often had to choose only four or five questions from as many as thirty-five) that 'question spotting' must surely be encouraged. Obviously, options are provided in order to allow both teacher an student greater flexibility in the selection of topics for 'in depth' study. Similarly, they provide a student with many opportunities to show what he *knows* rather than to reveal specific gaps in his knowledge of a given subject. Nevertheless, the large number of choices does encourage a fragmentary, anticipatory type of preparation that may do little to enhance one's understanding of history.

Similarly, there was little concern for the testing of one's understanding of broader historical movements or trends. In general, the questions seemed to deal largely with isolated pieces of history that implied a lack of concern for more comprehensive historical understanding.

I did not encounter any questions that required, say, reading a sample of historical writing, an original document, etc., and then *reacting* to it in some way. For example, while I often came across questions like, 'Give an account of the career and importance of Voltaire', students were seldom given a significant passage of Voltaire's and asked to react to it; perhaps responding first as individuals living in the twentieth century and then as members of the late eighteenth-century French nobility. In the same vein, students who were asked to 'Give four examples to show how nineteenth-century American novelists, poets or songwriters described contemporary events' could be exposed to excerpts from the songs, novels, or poems themselves and asked to suggest *when* they might have been written, why they were written, their significance, if any, etc. Occasionally students might be asked (for example) to suggest as many *possible* causes as they can think of to explain a given social phenomenon—or, to list the possible consequences of a real or hypothetical event. They might be asked to think through questions for which there is *no* 'right' answer (what would have happened if King Harold had won at Hastings? If the American colonies had lost the war for independence? If Hitler had postponed his invasion of Russia?). Or, they could be asked to evaluate a reproduction of, say, a Peter Breughel painting in terms of its value to modern man as an historical document.

Obviously, none of this can (or should) be done without a thorough re-evaluation of the purposes of history teaching at O level. At present it seems fair to say that the G.C.E. examination papers I reviewed reflected reasonably accurately the goals and objectives of the majority of the teachers of O level history with whom I came in contact.

Contrary to the opinion of many English critics of the examination system, I found that A level papers in history were, in many ways, a good deal 'better' (in my terms of reference) than were the O levels I examined. They still included, of course, dozens of the memory-convergent thinking sorts of questions that were criticized at O level. For example:

> What were the chief problems facing King John at his accession?
> What were the main considerations guiding papal policy towards England in this period?
> What efforts were made to reconcile the North and South before 1860?
> What factors advanced or retarded the process of Italian unification after 1848?

Similarly, classically vague questions (reminiscent of *1066 and All That*) continue to appear. For example:

> Was the disorder of Stephen's reign a reaction against anything?

As might be expected, A level questions dealt, in far greater detail, with an even narrower range of topics—which is, of course, consistent with the nature of A level history syllabuses in general. I found the same tendency to encourage 'question spotting' (a practice I observed first hand in a number of classrooms in which students were preparing for O and A levels) by asking students to choose, for example *four* questions out of *forty-one* options.

As with O levels, A level examinees must also work within rigid time limits, and one can only assume that the ability to bring forth a particular response within say, two hours, is valued more than certain other abilities, skills, or habits of work—even though historians themselves rarely apply (and sensibly so) such limitations to their own research.

In other ways, however, A level history papers seem to reflect the differing conceptions English educators hold of sixth form and pre-sixth form education which were discussed at some length earlier in this study.

I found, for example, a number of questions that asked students to evaluate or judge the *adequacy* of what we know rather than merely recall information. These are a few examples:

> What do you consider the decisive turning point in the history of the League of Nations?
>
> The inevitable outcome of government of the Directory was military dictatorship. Do you agree?
>
> Is it true to say that the major domestic problem facing the U.S.A. today, apart from the Negro problem, is automation?

Obviously, if teachers conceive of their function as providing one, specific, 'right' answer to questions like these, to be dutifully copied down in student notebooks—i.e., 'the decisive turning point in the history of the League of Nations was ——', then evaluative skills will *not* be called into play in the answering of such questions. However, if we can assume that other teaching strategies were employed, we might also assume that something more than memory would be involved in giving satisfactory answers to such questions.

I was similarly impressed with the sudden appearance of questions indicating that those studying history at A level were, at last, to become acquainted with the nature and method of history as a discipline. For example:

> Examine the view that 'history exists only in the mind of the historian'.

The defeat of the Anglo-Saxon Army at Hastings was tragic and complete, but that it happened was largely a matter of chance. Discuss.

Show the value to the social historian of either letters and diaries or drama in this period.

What are the main kinds of source material available for the study of King John's reign, and which do you consider the most illuminating?

How would you classify the sources of our information regarding Roman Britain?

Either discuss the evidence of Roman occupation in your locality *or* describe any 'dig' in which you have taken part.

Occasionally students are asked to react to specific examples of source material or to pertinent data that is actually included in the examination. One history paper on 'Economic and Public Affairs', for example, provides the following data and then asks the student to comment on its significance:

Comment upon these results of the 1959 General Election in Hertfordshire:

Constituency	Votes (to the nearest hundred)		
	Conservative	*Labour*	*Liberal*
East	28,200	18,000	7,700
Hertford	31,400	22,600	—
South-West	29,700	19,500	9,300
Barnet	33,100	19,700	—
Hemel Hempstead	30,200	22,000	8,400
Hitchin	30,200	25,800	8,500
St Albans	23,200	14,700	5,900
Total votes	206,000	142,300	40,800
%	53	37	10
Seats won	7	0	0

Still another question imaginatively asks that students 'write an obituary notice of Louis XIV as if written by either a contemporary Frenchman or a contemporary Dutchman'.

If one examines carefully the many 'special papers' that are used by universities to help select academically able students for honours courses, one finds even more searching questions. Consider, for example, the recent University of London special paper, reproduced in its entirety below:

HISTORY

Three hours

Answer three questions

Credit will be given for good English and the orderly presentation of material. Candidates who neglect these essentials will be penalized.

1. What do you regard as the major contributions made by the Middle Ages to European civilization?
2. Do you agree that 'there is altogether too much of kings and queens in our history books'?
3. Write a historical commentary on the notion of liberty.
4. Assess the importance of the knowledge of everyday things in understanding the main social trends of any period you have studied.
5. 'The revolt of Luther in 1517 marked the beginning of the modern world.' Discuss.
6. Examine the view that the nineteenth century was 'a period exuding confidence and optimism'.
7. How has the art of any period helped you to understand its history?
8. 'History is an art not a science.' Discuss.
9. Discuss the power of the press in modern society.
10. Consider from your knowledge of any period the view that 'civil wars leave deeper scars than the struggles of sovereign states'.
11. 'It is men's technological achievements, not their ideas, which set the pattern of society.' Examine this statement with reference to any period you have studied.
12. Assess the importance of non-written sources in the study of local history.

In summary then, one can only wonder (as an *American* observer) at the continued curricular 'narrowness' that dominates history teaching here which is, of course, reflected in examination questions at both A and O levels. The dichotomy between pre-sixth and sixth form conceptions of the nature of history itself (again, reflected quite clearly in the examination papers) is also difficult for me to accept, since it seems to rest upon certain assumptions about children's interests and abilities that are of exceedingly doubtful validity. Of course, the entire conception of evaluating two or more years of a student's work almost entirely on the basis of one externally administered examination seems to me to be indefensible, since it implies that the close contacts between teacher and pupil during this period—the insights, knowledge and understanding of a child that only a classroom teacher can have—are unimportant and relatively meaningless. As one perceptive teacher put it,

> I found that the really bright and shrewd boys did well in this as in every other exam—able people can work any system—but the less shrewd (and possibly more creative) pupils came unstuck in the exam, after an immensely enjoyable and valuable year's work on key aspects of history involving private research, wide reading, and some satisfying project work.

The G.C.E. in Geography

Both O and A level examinations in geography possess inherently some of the same negative qualities as do their counterparts in history. They must largely ignore, because they are externally administered, the 'local' evidence of achievement that may have accumulated during a student's study of geography in a given school. Similarly, the pressure of time is a factor in all G.C.E. examinations, and this too, as with history, places a considerable emphasis upon what may, in the final analysis, be an exceedingly irrelevant factor.

One also notices a marked (and not always justifiable) difference in the 'approach' to geography at pre- and post-sixth form levels which, again, merely reflects the attitudes held by those responsible for syllabus construction toward the nature, capacities and interests of fourteen- through seventeen- or eighteen-year-old children.

One finds, too, a similar emphasis at O level on questions requiring, essentially, the *recall* of information. For example:

> The following are on the steamship route from Britain to Tokyo. Insert (where necessary) and name: Mediterranean Sea, South China Sea, Suez Canal, Straits of Gibraltar, Aden, Bombay, Hong Kong, Naples, Singapore.

Children are expected to know and know quite thoroughly some region of Britain, as questions like this indicate:

> Draw a large sketch-map of the south-west peninsula (Cornwall, Devon, Dorset, Somerset). On it mark and name:
>
> 1. Bodmin Moor, Dartmoor, Exmoor, Mendip Hills.
> 2. The rivers Dart, Exe, Tamar, Parret.
> 3. Falmouth, Exeter, Plymouth, Taunton, Weymouth.

Detailed factual knowledge of a limited *local* area is also regularly tested:

> With reference to the British Isles, select one area of between one and five square miles of which you have *first hand knowledge*.
>
> (*a*) Name and locate it.
> (*b*) Draw a sketch-map to show its major geographical features.
> (*c*) Describe the relationship between two of these features.
> (*d*) Which of the features mapped are representative of the region of which your area is a part?

Obviously, in either history or geography it seems essential that students 'learn' a certain amount of factual, informational material. One cannot teach broad, over-arching concepts and generalizations exclusively. (Indeed, they would be meaningless without some factual illustrations to support them.) Neither can children engage wholly in creative or evaluative thinking. It struck me, however, as I viewed this type of question in both the history and geography examinations, that the geographer appeared to be asking children to 'learn' factual information that often seemed more significant, perhaps more meaningful, than did many of the 'facts' emphasized in O level history. This argument may be unfair because the geographer is essentially committed to the present, while the historian is, after all, concerned with the past. Nevertheless, I found it less difficult to quarrel with the notion that children should know the location of the Earth's major land masses and seas, or the basic physical make-up of their homeland, than with the assumption that one must 'know' why Frederick Barbarossa quarrelled with the Papacy.

On the other hand, the geographers, too, often asked for an encyclopedic kind of recall which would if successful, eliminate the need for a number of standard reference works. For example:

Show the *world distributions* (on the map provided) of coral, volcanoes, fjord coasts, and temperate deserts.

Draw a large sketch-map of Norway and Sweden. On it mark and name:

(i) Hardanger Fjold, Songe Fjord, River Glommen, Lake Wener, Lake Wetler.

(ii) Bergen, Oslo, Trondheim, Goteborg, Jankoping, Stockholm.

In any event, memorization questions obviously consume a large portion of O level geography papers, although I find the *type* of material memorized less objectionable in geography than in history.

The geography papers I examined also included, however, a number of questions designed to test something more than one's ability to recall information. For example, students might be provided with small, detailed ordnance survey maps at a scale, perhaps of one inch to the mile. They would then be expected to answer questions like these on the basis of the data contained on the map:

State the direction and distance by main road to the nearest quarter mile of the western end of the bridge over the River Torridge at 454264 from Northern School 449290.

Using evidence from the map suggest reasons for the importance of Bideford as a road junction.

Photographs were often provided in test booklets and were used as the 'raw material' for questions that rose considerably above the simple recall level. For example:

> The two pictures E and F are of the Canadian Prairies and the Polders of Holland respectively. Compare (i) the size of the fields and use of the land in E with those in F (ii) the settlements and roads shown in the two pictures. Suggest reasons for the differences you have mentioned.

Another question included photographs of a coral island, a desert, etc. Students were asked to 'describe the physical features shown in the photographs. Explain how any one of these features may have been formed.'

The geographers also tended to make more use at O level than did the historians of questions in which children were asked to *use* various data provided in the examination paper. These are representative of many similar questions which appeared in the papers I examined:

> Records of temperature and rainfall for three towns are given below. For *each* (a) write a description of the temperature and rainfall, (b) name the type of climate, giving reasons for your answer, (c) locate *one* area in the world where this type of climate occurs.

	J.	F.	M.	A.	My.	J.	Jy.	A.	S.	O.	N.	D.
A. (Alt. 9,350 ft.)												
Temp. (°F.)	55	55	55	55	55	55	55	55	55	55	54	55
Rainfall (in.)	3·2	3·9	4·8	7·0	4·6	1·5	1·1	2·2	2·6	3·9	4·0	3·6
B. (Alt. 30 ft.)												
Temp. (°F.)	44	44	45	48	52	57	59	59	57	52	48	46
Rainfall (in.)	5·5	5·2	4·5	3·7	3·2	3·2	3·8	4·8	4·1	5·6	5·5	6·6
C. (Alt. 64 ft.)												
Temp. (°F.)	78	79	81	84	88	92	95	94	92	89	86	81
Rainfall (in.)	1·5	0·6	0·6	0·8	0·0	0·0	0·0	0·0	0·0	0·3	0·7	1·4

I was less impressed, however, with the numbers of questions that literally forced children, by their wording, to accept a deterministic view of the world. Students were often asked to describe *exclusively physical* features which may encourage, say, the production of tea, coffee, wine, etc. While the physical environment does appear to set broad limits to the ways in which man uses the land, there are obviously dozens of other, largely cultural factors that play a part in the decision to raise a given product in a given place. The question does, of course, specify *physical* features which implies that *other* factors may be involved as well. However, I found *no* questions that specifically asked children to describe how man's *culture* has led two societies to use essentially the same land in entirely different ways. For example, a question like the following (while it has other weaknesses to which I will return later) *does* encourage (or at least *allows*) students to attack the population density problem in *broad* terms:

> Compare *the reasons* for the high density of population in either China or India and either North Eastern U.S.A. or Western Europe. [Italics mine.]

Other questions were really too big or too vague to handle— unless they were expected to be answered in an intentionally immature and inaccurate way. For example, children were asked to:

> Consult your atlas and then locate on sketch-maps *one* large region of the world with a high population density and one with a low population density. Explain these differences.

English geographers are well aware of the difficulty of using the population density concept over too large an area. Even New York State—a relatively small area—shows tremendous variations in population density as one moves from Manhattan Island to the heart of the Adirondack Mountains. These variations are easily masked by any large-scale density map, and, unless one is aware of its limitations, the concept is relatively useless. I can only assume that this is, perhaps, an example of a point of view expressed by a number of English geographer-educators (and treated in chapter IV). That is, 'it is alright to teach ideas, concepts or other information that may not be entirely accurate to children below the sixth form. They will simply have to learn what they can understand now and be retaught later when they are older and more ready to grasp the more subtle aspects of these understandings.'

At best, this is an uneconomical way to teach (and learn). Also, it assumes that complex ideas cannot be taught until an arbitrary age level has been reached—an obviously challenge-able assumption, in view of the success mathematicians (for example) have had in teaching set-theory to seven-year-olds. At worst, it leaves many children who will never take A level geography with a residue of inaccurate explanations for certain social or physical phenomena. As we said in the history section, an examination cannot be divorced from the syllabus it is supposed to examine. This appears to be an excellent example of an unfortunate kind of consistency.

Finally, one might mention again the considerable emphasis given in English geography examinations (and syllabuses) to questions dealing with material that would, in the U.S., be confined to geology courses. Questions like this, for example, would be unlikely to appear in an American geography paper at any level of instruction:

> On picture A place the appropriate letter on each of the following features: Lateral Moraine (L), Medial Moraine (M), Pyramidal Peak (P), Arête (A), Nevé (N), Glacier (G).

We find at A level a continued use of creative testing devices of all kinds that demand considerably more than the recall or memorization of factual information. A variety of photographs are used extensively as the raw data for questions requiring the *application* of previously acquired concepts, as the following question illustrates:

> Examine the three oblique areal photographs provided. Describe and attempt to explain the physical features shown in each of them.

Cartography gets increasing attention at A level, and again, students must demonstrate their grasp of important map-making skills by using them in completely new situations. For example:

TABLE OF COAL OUTPUT AND NUMBER OF UNDERGROUND
WORKERS AT TWELVE COLLIERIES IN THE LEICESTERSHIRE
DISTRICT OF ENGLAND (1961)

Colliery	Index Number on Outline Map (p. 5)	Output in 1,000 tons	Number of Underground Workers
Stanhope Bretby	1	90	140
Bretby	2	65	90
Cadley Hill	3	135	450
Church Gresley	4	300	700
Granville	5	275	490
Rawdon	6	650	940
Donisthorpe	7	720	875
Measham	8	400	500
Snibston	9	400	650
South Leicester	10	270	525
Bagworth	11	290	375
Desford	12	655	960

(a) *On the outline map on page* 5, represent by *different* cartographical
methods:
    (i) The coal output of *each* colliery.
    (ii) The output of coal per underground worker at *each*
       colliery.
(b) *In your answer book*, comment on the merits and the limitations
of the two different methods employed by you in (a).

In contrast to American practice, *physical* geography is given a great deal of attention, and questions in this area demand a detailed knowledge of geomorphology that indicates quite clearly the highly specialized nature of secondary school geography in England. The following illustrative questions (the student does not have to answer *all* of them) comprise the section on 'The Land' in the London Board's *Physical Geography* paper:

1. By reference to specific areas, distinguish between the effects of intrusive and extrusive igneous activity on the surface features of the earth.
2. Using actual examples, discuss the form and origin of *four* landforms characteristic of a glaciated or formerly glaciated mountain area.
3. With the aid of diagrams and sketch-maps, assess the relative importance of water and wind in the formation of desert landforms.
4. By reference to specific areas, discuss the nature and origin of landforms that would help you to recognize karst in the field.
5. *Either* describe some field-work you have carried out in connection with your study of landforms, illustrating your answer with maps and sketches.
   Or explain, with the aid of maps and diagrams, the main features of not more than 15 miles of coastline which you have studied in detail on maps and/or in the field.

We find also at A level a sudden emphasis on the concept of regionalization, and sixth formers are unhesitatingly asked to *create* and *justify* regional divisions of given areas. The concept of regionalization as an *arbitrary* delimitation from other areas, i.e., as an intellectual judgment based upon one's choice of the specific criteria chosen to delimit one area from another, gets considerable emphasis here—while pre-A level students deal with the concept of 'region' in both syllabus *and* examination as a fixed and somehow pre-determined division of the land. This then, is still another example of the tendency here to *assume* that certain ideas—often those vital to a mature understanding of a given discipline—simply must wait until one does A level work or, perhaps, until one reads his subject at a university. This is not to suggest that Bruner is 100 per cent correct in his challenging assertion that 'any subject can be taught effectively in some intellectually honest form to any child at any stage of development'.[1] However—and to the surprise of hundreds of educators both in the U.S. and elsewhere—Bruner's notion, when adequately developed and tested in the classroom, is apparently more right than wrong. Indeed, the safest position one might take today is that we are really only *beginning* to find out what can and cannot be taught to children at various age levels. Surely if two-year-olds can be taught to read (admittedly with the use of quite complex electronic equipment) we might at least consider the possibility that fourteen-year-olds can be taught concepts like regionalization in a way that will not require un-learning or re-teaching at a later date.

Similarly, one finds questions in A level geography papers that seem to deal with the *human* factors that effect man's use of his physical environment. Contrast, for example, the following questions with the related O level questions mentioned above:

> How far does the one-inch map extract enable you to understand the growth and present significance of the town of Ludlow? What *other* information would you require to extend your understanding of Ludlow? [Italics mine.]
>
> *It is usually insufficient to explain the distribution of population in terms of physical geography alone.* [Italics mine.] Discuss this statement by reference to one continent you have studied.

One can only applaud the implications of such questions and wonder why it is that they appear so rarely in geography examination papers other than those at A level.[2]

The Certificate of Secondary Education

Approximately the 'top' 20 per cent of England's secondary school students take the G.C.E. examinations. The C.S.E. was created in order to provide an examination suitable for the next 20 per cent, and therefore enable these children (presumably) to share at least to some extent in the status that seems

---

[1] J. Bruner, *The Process of Education*, New York: Vintage Books, 1963, p. 33.

[2] It should be noted that the Oxford and Cambridge Boards are planning to introduce in 1968 a new A level examination in geography that will correct at least some of the weaknesses discussed in this chapter.

to come (in England) with success in passing a nationally recognized examination. While it is expected that employers will use C.S.E. results in selecting job applicants, it is also assumed that the examination will provide some evidence of a student's suitability for some form of further education. Similarly, since the C.S.E. tests the work done in a given subject over the *whole five years* of secondary education, there are hopes that it will, therefore, encourage more students to stay in school at least until the age of sixteen.

It should be mentioned at the outset that the C.S.E., unlike the G.C.E. provides schools with three examination plans, i.e., a school may elect to study the regionally, externally created syllabus and take its examination, *or*, it may create a local syllabus but request an external examination by a regional board, *or* it may examine (with regional examining board supervision) its own, locally constructed syllabus.

Obviously, this creates the possibility for a good deal of local option in syllabus construction and examining; an opportunity, if you will, for the critics of the 'evils' of G.C.E. to stop talking and start actively creating syllabuses and examinations that will better suit their own, particular local conditions. Whether or not teachers and headmasters will avail themselves of this opportunity in any appreciable number is difficult to say at this time.

Another C.S.E. innovation is described in the Southern Regional Examinations Board Syllabus for 1965:

> As an alternative to one question on Part II of the written paper the examination of an *individual assignment* done as *course work* will be accepted. It is hoped that local history will inspire most of the projects thus attempted.
>
> Another alternative accepted in place of one question on Part II of the paper will be a *research topic* to be completed under supervision in the Library or History Room using recommended reference books, a list of which will be sent to schools notifying the Board of their intention of accepting this alternative. Such schools will be required to select the research topic from the topics listed in Part II (Section C) of the written paper. Candidates exercising this choice will not be allowed to answer any question from this same topic on the Part II written paper.

Here obviously is an attempt to provide, as a part of the

external, regional examination itself, opportunities for the evaluation of 'project' and other work done *during* the preceding years by an individual student at a given school.

Other general changes might be noted as well; for example, the tendency to include 'objective' questions such as true-false, multiple choice and sentence completion, or short, written answers consisting of a sentence or a brief paragraph, *rather* than rely largely on essay questions. However, it might prove more valuable at this point to examine C.S.E. papers in history, geography and social studies in particular.

C.S.E. History

Since, as has been said before, examinations generally reflect rather closely the emphases and biases of the syllabuses they are designed to test, one will quickly notice the greater attention C.S.E. examinations give to more recent history and to social and economic history. In most cases, then, the material itself that is to be examined appears to consist of historical 'stuff' that should be more palatable for most adolescents. Similarly, since some use *is* made of the assessments of classroom teachers concerning a child's work during the preceding years' study, we might assume that the results obtained might ultimately reveal a more accurate picture of the achievement of a given pupil.

Other positive factors (to this observer, at least) were the appearance of a number of questions that were considerably broader and more general in nature; questions that allow for comparison and evaluation. For example:

(*a*) Compare the way you spend your leisure time in 1965 with the way you might have spent it had you been alive in 1905.

(*b*) Compare the standard of living of a working-class family in 1905 with the same type of family today.

What do you think were the three most important inventions or improvements in industry or agriculture in the period 1760–1830? Give reasons for your answer.

This question surely encourages a student to apply what he knows in a unique situation for which there can be no preconceived, 'set' answers:

> Imagine you are a 'backbencher'. Describe a bill you would like to introduce in Parliament. Explain the procedure to do this and the difficulties you would be likely to meet.

A cursory look at a group of C.S.E. history papers usually reveals a more attractive appearance than their rather grim, workmanlike G.C.E. counterparts. One notices a good many maps, for example, as well as charts and graphs of various kinds. These appearances are, however, often deceiving. Maps are generally used as the basis for questions involving simple location rather than for more complex or creative activities, e.g., 'identify a country that has left the Commonwealth'. (One teacher whose classroom I visited had displayed two large political maps of Africa; the first created about 1925, the second in 1964. The unique data provided so visually by the two maps served as the basis for a lesson in which each student was to produce a hypothetical map of 'Africa in 1984', making whatever changes he felt would be appropriate and, of course, *justifying* his projected image on the basis of historical as well as other information. The utilization of maps in this way, i.e., to encourage more complex, more creative thinking, occurred rarely, if at all.)

Similarly, one cannot help but notice the overwhelming number of questions that depend completely on simple recall or memory—the kinds of questions that concern so many English critics of examinations—and the kinds of questions that one hoped would be kept to a minimum in C.S.E. examinations. For example:

> Give a short account of any two of the following. Say what caused them and how the government tried to deal with them.
>
> (*a*) The Luddite riots.
> (*b*) The march of the Blanketeers.
> (*c*) The Peterloo massacre.
> (*d*) The Cato Street Conspiracy.

> An Antarctic explorer who died while on an expedition was:
> Fridtjof Nansen.
> Robert Scott.
> Edmund Hillary.
> Admiral Byrd.

The International Geophysical Year was:
1952.
1956.
1957–58.
1961–62.

The major sea battle of the First World War was fought at:
Gallipoli.
River Somme.
River Marne.
Jutland.

What took place on 6th June 1944?

Who was 'old Noll' and what were his 'ironsides'?

As might be expected, there is little or no attention paid to history as a discipline—to its strengths and weaknesses, its methods, the ways in which it utilizes data from the other social sciences, the sorts of questions historians ask about man and society as opposed to those the geographer (and others) ask, etc. Similarly, the C.S.E. examinations had their full quota of overly broad, impossible-to-answer-in-twenty-minutes questions, as well as selection problems that would, again, enable one to score well on the exam with only a piecemeal, disjointed knowledge of history.

In summary, then, one might conclude that while the C.S.E. in history surely opens up new possibilities for improving examining procedures in England, at this writing it has not lived up to the expectations of those who have read the statements of goals and objectives that appear in the C.S.E. publications.

C.S.E. Geography

Surely students thumbing through typical C.S.E. geography papers at the beginning of an examination must feel somewhat relieved and psychologically reassured. There are many blank spaces; sketches, diagrams, charts, and tables abound and it almost looks as if it might be fun to take the test. One certainly gets the impression that more practical, perhaps more 'relevant' aspects of geography are about to be tested, and (apart from the less effective use made of photographs compared to O level G.C.E. papers) I think this is essentially true. The C.S.E. tests surely seem less picayune, less narrow. The number of questions emphasizing factual recall ('The average rainfall in London is ————.') are kept under control, and time is left, therefore, for attention to local field work, aspects of literary geography, and a goodly number of 'why', 'how' and 'so what' questions. The examinations still appear to be disjointed and fragmentary; they sometimes seem condescendingly simple; occasionally a map or chart seems to be included simply as a visual stimulus rather than as a means of getting at important understandings that cannot be examined in any other way; 'determinism' and physical geography still hold sway; nevertheless, I was impressed with these papers—particularly so with the following questions:

This is an extract from a B.O.A.C. timetable.

Hong Kong	departure	18:00 Thursday
Tokyo	arrival	21:45
	departure	22:45
Honolulu	arrival	11:05 Thursday
	departure	12:30
San Francisco	arrival	20:15

How is it that a passenger on this service seems to reach San Francisco $2\frac{1}{4}$ hours after he left Hong Kong, which is 6,900 miles away?

Why was the St Lawrence Seaway thought necessary?

The 'Dust Bowl' of Nebraska and Colorado has been called a 'man-made' desert. Explain this statement.

On the map provided (a Mercator projection) pencil two *air* routes, one from London to a town in South America and one from London to a town in Australia.

How has the discovery of oil affected the daily life of an Arab or Kuwait?

These are, of course, merely random samples of what seemed to me to be searching, significant questions. The papers I examined were fairly liberally sprinkled with such items. Given the other advantages listed earlier, there seems every possibility that C.S.E. geography may have a considerable and positive impact on English education.

C.S.E. Social Studies

Much of what has been said elsewhere about 'social studies' in general undoubtedly applies to the C.S.E. papers I reviewed.

That is, the questions tend usually to deal with 'practical', current, 'relevant' problems involved in everyday living—whether or not they have much relation to social science. Some of the syllabuses represent far too ambitious programs for the relatively short periods of time that are allotted to them—again, apparently, reflecting the view that most of this material is largely 'common sense' and, therefore, does not require either a systematic approach or a large amount of a student's time. (Incidentally, at this writing, at least half of the Regional Examining Boards did *not* see social studies as important enough to warrant the creation of syllabuses or examinations in that area, although *all* of them offer history and geography.)

If the following statement of aims for a C.S.E. social studies course is at all typical (and I think it is) one should not find it terribly difficult to predict the nature of the questions likely to appear on C.S.E. social studies papers.

The syllabus is intended to provide an opportunity to develop responsibility and initiative in individual children; to increase their self-respect; to provide the incentive and to foster the ability to be of service to the Community and to develop a critical faculty in relation to environment.

This may be achieved by relating studies to the life and activities of the locality, the country and the world. Whenever possible, studies should be linked with events of current significance. Every attempt should be made to see that pupils are introduced to real situations, especially locally, where they can obtain first-hand knowledge of the world of work. Particular reference should be made to the relative roles of the adolescent and adult in a working environment. The studies outlined should be of direct service to the pupils in planning their leisure and work and in accepting their civic and moral responsibilities as citizens in the society of the future.

In general, I think it would be fair to say that an examination of existing C.S.E. social studies papers reveals a fascinating potpourri of items running the gamut from those that might be described as searching and intellectually demanding to something quite the opposite. Obviously, few patterns have been established here as yet. The examiners are apparently struggling to make the papers 'easy' and 'practical' enough to suit their conceptions of the abilities of those that will take the C.S.E., as well as 'difficult' enough (i.e., enough like the

G.C.E.) so that the examinations will gain some sort of status among the public-at-large.

For example, I felt the following questions were good ones, and refreshingly unlike most of those one is accustomed to seeing at O level in the G.C.E.—particularly in history.

The paragraph which follows has been taken from a novel dealing with life in the South African city of Johannesburg. Read it carefully and answer *all* the questions.

'. . . Yes, I have a room that I would let, but I do not want to let it. I have only two rooms and there are six of us already, and the boys and girls are growing up. But school books cost money and my husband is ailing and when he is well it is only thirty-five shillings a week. And six shillings of that is for the rent, and three shillings for travelling and a shilling that we may be buried decently, and a shilling for the books, and three shillings is for clothes . . . and a shilling for my husband's beer . . . and a shilling for sickness, that leaves seventeen shillings for food for six, and we are always hungry.'

(a) How many children are there in the family?
(b) What do you learn about the schools in Johannesburg?
(c) Why do you think the mother had to save each week towards doctor's fees and burial expenses?
(d) How large is the average family in England?
(e) How do you think a typical housewife in Britain might describe her weekly budget?

An old lady, who had spent her life in the East End, was heard to say:

'People today are not so neighbourly. They cannot be bothered to come and talk to you or afford to mix up and have a good chat. Some people who have got on better than you cannot be bothered with you. You used to get people saying good night and all the family used to pop in, even cousins. Now they are out in the New Towns.'

After reading the above extract very carefully, answer the following questions:

(a) 'People today are not so neighbourly.' Give your reasons for agreeing or disagreeing with this statement.
(b) Whom do you think she meant by 'all the family'?
(c) 'People cannot be bothered to come and talk to you.' Why do you think they could not bother to talk to her?
(d) What differences do you think the people going to the New Towns will find there?

Study the following chart:

Age Group	Percentage distribution of population of England and Wales	
	1951	*1961*
0–4	8·5	7·8
5–9	7·2	7·1
10–14	6·4	8·1
15–24	12·9	13·1
25–34	14·5	12·7
35–44	15·3	13·6
45–54	13·7	14·0
55–64	10·4	11·7
65–74	7·5	7·6
75 and over	3·6	4·3
All ages	100·0	100·0

From these figures, answer the following:

(*a*) Which age groups have increased since 1951?
(*b*) Which age groups have declined?
(*c*) What implications have these figures for the future so far as the social services are concerned?
(*d*) Suggest why more people are living longer nowadays.
(*e*) Suggest three problems the increasing population will bring.

Describe the social conditions and background from which any *one* group of coloured immigrants to this country come. What problems may they face when they reach and settle in Great Britain?

What do we mean by a 'group' in Social Studies?

List two small and two large groups to which you belong.

In a paragraph describe the role of the father *or* mother in *either* an English family *or* a family in another culture.

Name three ways in which man is superior to the animals and say briefly why these advantages have made him superior.

Describe three important skills a child must learn before he can live as an accepted member of society.

State three ways in which a child learns these skills.

Here is a list of problems from which an elderly person may suffer. Using each as a heading, write paragraphs to indicate how you think these problems may be relieved.

S.S.E.E.—12

(*a*) Loneliness.
(*b*) Boredom.
(*c*) Poverty.
(*d*) Poor accommodation.

On the other hand, questions calling for the recall of isolated factual material ('what Acts of Parliament are concerned with the safety and well-being of industrial workers?') continued to appear, as did questions that seemed to me to be condescendingly simple ('which party won the last general election?').

Similarly, one is likely to find questions appearing on C.S.E. social studies papers dealing with anything from advertising to 'hire purchase'. This is merely a reflection, of course, of the type of 'catch-all' syllabus created largely for school leavers and less able students that we have come to associate with 'social studies' in England. Until 'social studies' becomes more clearly and precisely defined (and, hopefully, more closely associated with social *science*), we may expect to find that C.S.E. syllabuses and examinations will continue to serve as repositories for those 'relevant', 'practical', and 'useful' topics that seem so often to serve as substitutes for a systematic study of man and society.

Eleven Plus Selection

If your child is one of the great majority of pupils who are going to make use of the public system of education, let him feel that there is no reason for fussing about the fact that a decision will be made as to whether he will be offered a selective grammar place commencing in September 1966. By all means give him a bicycle or whatever else is his heart's desire, but do not offer it on condition that he 'passes'! If he should be selected for a grammar place let him enjoy his 'success' but do not let him think he is superior to children who have not been selected. If he is not selected, do not allow him to be discouraged or to think he is 'below average'. He very likely is not below average because one has to be above average to be selected for a grammar place.

The preceeding paragraph was part of a letter from Surrey's 'Chief Education Officer' which was mailed to the parents of children about to take the eleven plus examination in that county. I leave it to the reader to place himself imaginatively in the role of a parent whose child has *not* passed the examination. He may then assess for himself the degree of comfort he might take from the Chief Education Officer's interpretations of the meaning of 'success', 'failure', 'pass', 'superior', or 'below-average'.

In any event it is not my purpose to deal at any length with the pros and cons of eleven plus selection in this study. Nevertheless, at this writing, many English children still go through some form of selection at about age eleven, and we shall confine ourselves largely to a consideration of the affects of eleven plus selection on social studies teaching in primary schools.

Unlike private preparatory schools in which history and geography appear to have equal status with mathematics and English, these subjects are perceived as 'second class' and relatively unimportant by both teachers and children in many maintained schools. It could hardly be otherwise, since the Common Entrance Examination includes *compulsory* papers in history and geography as well as English, mathematics, French, Latin and Scripture, while the eleven plus does not.

In some schools, one notices a more or less 'even' neglect of social studies in the curriculum at *all* age levels. (This is not to imply, incidentally, that some form of history, geography, or environmental studies is not carried out at *all* in such schools. We are speaking here of the *relative* neglect of these studies when compared to the time and attention given to, say, mathematics and English.)

In other schools, social studies are given some reasonable amount of curricular attention *until* children reach age ten. Then learning becomes a series of mathematics, English and even intelligence test 'drills' or exercises in order to prepare for the impending examinations.

Some headmasters refuse to be intimidated by the eleven plus and continue to offer broad, challenging curricula, neglecting neither music or art, science or social studies. When the examination comes it comes, and it is simply taken in stride as part of a school day or week. (The Oxfordshire schools discussed more completely in chapter II would be an excellent example.) Other systems (Leicestershire, for example) have developed non-selective secondary education patterns, and the positive effects of this lack of pressure on lower school teachers and headmasters is immediately observable as one visits Leicestershire primary schools. Where selection still exists, however, the social studies (as well as certain other subjects) are, with rare exceptions, seriously neglected.

Interestingly enough, so-called 'informational subjects' have been excluded from the eleven plus historically in order *not* to discriminate against children whose home backgrounds might not contribute as fully to a child's broader education as would others. The assumption was, apparently, that by testing only the 'basic skills' one might considerably eliminate social class bias in selection. That fallacy has been dramatically exposed by English sociologists however, and much of the current criticism of the examination rests on evidence indicating that it is in the area of the use and comprehension of spoken *language* that lower class children are truly at a disadvantage when compared to their middle and upper class counterparts.

In other words, most English educators (however reluctantly) *are* coming to the conclusion that the eleven plus examination is inherently unfair and biased in favor of middle and upper class children. Therefore, the 'curricular price' that many English primary schools have been paying in order to prepare their children for an examination that now appears to be of dubious validity would seem to be, in my opinion, far too high to justify its continued use.

Some General Comments Concerning the Role of Examinations in English Education

The Surrey County Council Education Committee justifies its selective system of education with phrases like this:

> Some of the ablest children, however, will need even at the early age of eleven to go to a school providing more advanced academic education, so there has to be a selection procedure. . . .[1]

Most Americans, on the other hand, from Jefferson to Mann, Dewey and Cremin would insist that the '*general* diffusion of'

[1] Surrey County Council Education Committee. *Secondary Education in Surrey*. Kingston-Upon-Thames, 1966, p. 3.

knowledge rather than the liberal education of leaders should be the paramount concern of a republican society'.[1] Given this dichotomy of beliefs and assumptions, it is difficult indeed to react objectively to the concept of selective education in general and, of course, the elaborate examination system implied in the acceptance of such a system. This is not to say that examinations of all kinds do not play an ever-increasing role in American education; they *do*. Surely the taking of College Boards by an American sixteen- or seventeen-year-old must be as traumatic an experience as is the sitting of A or O levels by an English youngster. Yet, the relative open-endedness, the relative 'looseness' of American secondary education does tend to both play down the importance of any specific examination (although *not* the importance of examinations in general) as well as postpone until much later in a child's life the really crucial, career-determining decisions that will be made with the help of examinations of various types.

Criticism, then, comes easily when one is evaluating the efficiency of a device, the basic function or purpose of which is disapproved of to begin with. Nevertheless, one must react as honestly as one can, and the following conclusions may perhaps be of some interest and value to both English and American readers.

To begin with, the English examination system *does* give a degree of stability to English education that may be lacking in America. G.C.E. requirements remain more or less constant regardless of 'teacher turnover', and education here does seem to be happily free from the fads that periodically seem to effect American education.

Similarly, while both G.C.E. and C.S.E. are 'national' exams, one has nine G.C.E. boards to choose from as well as a continuing option to develop new syllabuses for Board approval so that individualism does not *need* to suffer under the English system.

On the other hand, the evidence is that despite the lack of 'centralization', despite the possibilities for individualization that exist, English secondary schools rarely go out on new curricular limbs. For example, out of 1600 schools examined

---

[1] L. Cremin, *The Genius of American Education*. Pittsburgh: University of Pittsburgh Press, 1965, p. 42.

by the London Board (offering ten subjects each) only *ten* special subject papers were submitted.[1] Special, 'local' syllabuses simply were *not* being developed in anything approaching substantial numbers—although the option to do so has always existed.

If the winds of change blow only mildly from *outside* the examination establishment, there is a veritable calm *within* the system. Syllabuses and examinations respond slowly to the pressures of new developments and discoveries in the various disciplines; indeed, the pace at which significant revisions in G.C.E. history and geography take place has been described by some English educators as 'glacier-like' with even minor reforms taking five years or so to implement.

The pressures for examination success can lead in England (as well as in America) to educationally indefensible cramming: to situations, for example, where a boy or girl who has taken a given A level examination spends an entire year going over the *same* material in hopes of obtaining a higher grade. Obviously, 'learning for learning's sake' which is difficult to achieve under the most ideal conditions becomes close to impossible to achieve when so much depends upon examination successes, and students who devote themselves to the study of a subject largely for the intrinsic rewards involved in such study are rare indeed.

To put similar pressures on primary children through the medium of the eleven plus examination seems even less defensible. Even if one ignored the considerable evidence indicating that the eleven plus is exceedingly 'culture-bound' and discriminates against lower-class children the effects of such examinations upon both curriculum and teaching at this level should make this procedure highly questionable.

The general effects of a fairly rigid examination system on children's attitudes, motivation and self-concept are difficult to measure in any truly objective way. Perceptive teachers and headmasters have written eloquently, however, of their observations of the effects of 'the system' on their children. Perhaps such comments may say more than would the inclusion of additional coldly statistical research data. This, for example,

[1] R. J. Montgomery, *Examinations*. London: Longmans, Green and Co. Limited. 1965, p. 178.

was written by a primary teacher on the eve of the 'eleven plus day':

It is a black day. Nervous children foredoomed to failure as certain as night follows this day will sit tense in their seats tomorrow, their visions obscured by the glimpses of promised bicycles, train sets, and even ponies, dripping slowly away in the torture of irrelevant questions. They are certain failures because the grammar school will only take four at the most from my class, and I have known who they will be for two years. That is, as long as I have been teaching at this school.

I remember the dismal evenings when the parents were consulted. How should I advise a mother who has already bought her daughter's grammar school uniform that Patricia is at least fifteenth in line for the four places, although she is above average in intelligence? How do I tell her without sounding crude and patronizing, that Patricia is a gifted mixer and is friends with everyone? Socially she heads any list, but the eleven plus will call her a failure.

Stephen is an eleven-year-old artist in paint and clay. His fingers have fashioned a clay snake charmer this week which actually breathes. He is a walking ornithological encyclopedia. Can you describe an avocet and draw one accurately? Stephen can. He writes touching prose in a beautiful italic hand. He never hears what I am saying, thank God, his head is too full of ideas. He will be called a failure tomorrow.[1]

---

[1] This appeared in the *Guardian* on 8th March 1966, p. 11.

VIII: SUMMARY AND CONCLUSIONS

T HE PERENNIAL danger of evaluating aspects of a given nation's system of education by the standards of another is very real indeed. It is only fair, then, that one 'declare one's interest' (as I have already done), face up to the reality that one may indeed be *wrong*, and then proceed to evaluate on the basis of one's admittedly and unavoidably biased perceptions.

Having so warned the reader, let me say at once that there is (as I perceive it) much that is 'good' and much that is 'bad' in the social education of English children. I hope I have been alert enough to see that a good deal of the 'bad' is attributable to forces over which professional educators have little or no control. Headmasters and teachers, for example, cannot solve Britain's recurring economic difficulties, nor can they undo the physical damage to her cities wrought during World War II, change the conditions that have encouraged the immigration of large numbers of 'different' people from Commonwealth nations who have chosen to live in English cities and attend English schools, or create a less mobile, more stable society that would minimize educational problems. English educators (*and* their American counterparts) face both unique and herculean tasks at this particular moment in history and, as is so often the case, there is very little precedent upon which to base the decisions which will effect the lives of millions of children. Nevertheless, teachers, headmasters, and others *have* and *are* making such decisions and, having acknowledged the problems that beset them, we are still faced with the task of evaluating what they have done.

Let us look first at a number of factors which I perceive as 'good':

1. One cannot spend even a few weeks in England without becoming aware of the 'open-ness', the atmosphere of political

tolerance, that exists in virtually all aspects of English life. American schools, with all of their traditional emphases on 'citizenship education', have never been able to develop a political climate as accepting of divergency as is the English. The degree to which the schools are responsible for this condition is, of course, uncertain. (Similarly, American schools cannot shoulder all of the blame for the political intolerance that often mars our history.) Certainly, one sees little direct attention paid to the achievement of so valued a goal. Nevertheless, the school is in England, as it is elsewhere, one of society's chief socializing agents, and we must assume that schools *do* play a role in developing the kind of citizen who is willing to allow all views to be heard, no matter how obnoxious they may be to him personally.

2. In the best of England's primary schools, a degree of individual freedom, flexibility and (eventually) responsibility exists in a way that is virtually unknown in most American elementary schools. Surely this total school atmosphere or climate makes significant contributions to the social education of children who are exposed to it, and while little 'data' exists that might measure the achievements of such schools with precision, one's observation of children at work or at play, as individuals or in groups, leads one to the inescapable conclusion that these schools *are* playing a significant role in the development of the sorts of traits and abilities that seem crucial to the 'enlightened' citizen of a truly democratic society. One must reluctantly point out, however, that such schools are very much in the minority, even though many headmasters give lip-service to these broad educational aims.

3. In a more narrow sense, social studies teachers in a number of countries might learn a great deal from their English counterparts about creative and challenging ways to use the local environment as a vital part of the social education of children and youth. In school after school I saw teachers and their students using the fields, farms, buildings and people which surround them in a way few American teachers do. Similarly, the rigor with which geographical field studies are carried out is impressive, as is the thoroughness of the teaching of physical geography in general.

4. While few American educators would advocate either a

highly selective system of education *or* the early subject-matter specialization that seems so typical of most of England's 'selective' schools, it seems nevertheless that we might profit a great deal from studying the ways in which academically able 'historians', 'geographers' and 'social scientists' are taught in English sixth forms. It might well be possible to adopt some of the positive elements of the sixth form without necessarily converting to a selective system of education. Similarly, one would hope that efforts would be made to retain many of these practices as England moves more and more rapidly towards a system of comprehensive secondary education. Surely the many illustrations of excellence at this level of English education contained in the proceding chapters should justify considerable interest among American social studies teachers.

5. At best, English children and youth (through their ubiquitous community service programs) become involved with and learn a great deal about the problems, needs, and aspirations of a variety of groups that are often grossly neglected in other societies. While such programs cannot and should not be construed as substitutes for systematic classroom study, they do nevertheless, provide significant learning experiences for a great many English children.

6. While integrated, cross-disciplinary courses in social studies have never really caught on in England to the extent that they have in the United States, there is nevertheless, a significant 'stirring' going on in this field—and the people who are involved in such work seem to me to be among England's most talented teachers and scholars. They have, therefore, created a number of courses of study that because of their quality and uniqueness (rather than their numbers) are deserving of careful study and analysis by American (and other) educators.

So much for the 'good' in English social education. Much more could have been said and, indeed, much more has been said in the seven chapters that preceded this one. Nevertheless, our task here is not to catalogue specifics but rather to outline a few broad, positive practices and achievements that might warrant considerable thought and study by those concerned with the social education of children. Let us now attempt a similar analysis of the 'bad'.

1. There seems to be in England a continuing (though declining) suspicion of the academic respectability of the social sciences as worthwhile vehicles for study in schools. Traditionally, history and geography have been perceived as the most effective means of helping a child understand his world, and it is only recently that elements of sociology, political science, anthropology and economics have found their way into the school curriculum. Obviously, if one accepts the notion that these disciplines are indeed important; that one cannot understand the modern world in any real sense without some understanding of them—then their neglect in English social studies curricula represents a significant weakness.

2. Ian Lister once commented that 'we (in England) must acknowledge that the very liberty, flexibility and variety of the educational structure have ensured that experiment should be limited and isolated, and have often encouraged tribalism in educational organization and staunch conservatism in educational practice'.[1] There are then, evils in diversity as well as strengths. One of those evils is surely the relative haphazardness of curricular development in general, the lack of mutual attacks on mutual problems, the tendency to 'go it alone', blithely unaware of what others are doing, the tendency (often because of the lack of broader, better manned and better financed projects) to neglect the spelling out of goals and procedures or the creation of adequate teaching materials. One might say that a good deal is left to 'faith' and—in curriculum development as in other fields—faith *alone* often proves an inadequate solution to our problems.

3. In general, it seems that far too little attention is paid to the problem of broadly evaluating the outcomes of social education *other* than mastery of factual information. This is particularly apparent when a school tries out a new 'experimental' program or curriculum. Whether or not pupils *are* developing certain attitudes, concepts, skills, interests, etc., is seldom determined, and teachers seem mostly to be unaware that techniques do indeed exist for the measurement of the more subtle (yet

[1] J. H. Plumb, Editor, *Crisis in the Humanities*. London: Penguin Books, 1964, p. 166.

possibly more important) goals of courses in social studies. Similarly, teachers make little use of such techniques to diagnose children's educational needs in these fields. On the other hand (and quite paradoxically) many English educators display a great faith in the ability of examinations to 'sort children out' for assignment to given schools or 'streams', even though there is considerable research indicating that the kinds of abilities usually measured on such tests are not necessarily indicative of a child's ability to think creatively about social problems, evolve or develop a generalization on the basis of certain data, or to apply his understanding of a given concept to a new situation.

4. Closely related to this point, of course, is the general lack of concern for the teaching of the methods of the social scientist as an integral and significant part of a social studies or related course.

5. Perhaps one of the most significant problems that I observed was the tendency to avoid areas of social conflict, unpleasantness, or controversy in history, geography or other courses—particularly below the sixth form. The role that the social studies curriculum *might* play in breaking down class barriers, in building respect for and understanding of minority groups in English society, in encouraging a reasoned approach to the analysis of social problems of all kinds, seems largely to be ignored.

6. There tends to be among many English educators a dangerous tendency to polarize curricular views; to see curriculum revision and improvement as a matter of either juggling required topics or subjects that *must* be 'covered', or, as a continued pressure to loosen the reins, teach whatever seems to be of interest to children, thus eliminating requirements or structure of any kind, and, in general, adopting a completely laissez-faire approach. Most American educators would probably accept the notion that it is absolutely essential to teach the child *within a framework of societal and cultural* significance— and that we do so without violating what we know about the great variety and complexity of the differences that exist among children. That is, *what* we study does make a difference; while the words 'societal and cultural significance' are open to *broad* interpretation, they are not open to *unlimited* interpretation.

Obviously, this calls for a concerted attempt to create such a framework and identify significant concepts, generalizations, attitudes, and skills. So far this task has been seriously neglected in English curriculum work in the social studies.

And so much, then, for the 'bad'. Quite obviously, some of the objections I have raised, some of the approaches I have criticized will be viewed by English educators as relatively unimportant, irrelevant, or perhaps as strengths rather than as weaknesses. This is, of course, the chance one takes when one criticizes an aspect or institution of a given society from within the cultural borders of his own. I would like therefore to conclude this study with a list of *questions* rather than with a series of more or less dogmatic statements about what may be 'good' or 'bad' in the social education of English children. They are not meant to be inclusive; rather, they seem to me to be representative of the kinds of questions English teachers and headmasters ought to ask more frequently than they do; the kinds of questions that will need to be answered before really effective curriculum revision in the social studies can take place in England.

1. There has been a very real 'explosion of knowledge' in the social sciences. This is more than a cliché; it can be documented in a thousand ways, and it shows every sign of rapid acceleration during the years ahead. Only the simplest of societies can hope to teach its children 'all they need to know', i.e., to 'cover' a field. Certainly there is no possibility of 'covering' the myriad of people, events, and movements that comprise the discipline of history alone, to say nothing of geography, anthropology, economics, political science and sociology. Therefore it has become increasingly important to ask, what knowledge is of the most worth to *our* society at this particular moment in time? Which ideas will help the non-specialist citizen to understand the world in which he lives? Which ideas are fundamental enough to have transfer value, i.e., which ideas will help one to better understand a unique social phenomenon that has not been formally studied before? If we accept the fact that we cannot teach *everything*, on what bases *do* we select what must be studied, and, of equal importance how do we organize this material for study?

2. As more and more children stay in school for longer and longer periods of time we will have to come to grips with the problem of creating sequential, coordinated curricula in the social studies. English educators must, then, ask themselves whether the laying out of a planned, sequential curriculum dealing perhaps, with primary *and* secondary education in a given town or city is necessarily 'undemocratic' or unfaithful to our knowledge of child development. Can each school continue to go its own way? Is there a need for some sort of 'common core' of experience for all or most children?

3. As one examines the dichotomy that apparently exists between teaching procedures and goals in pre-sixth form work and in sixth forms, i.e., the tendency to view the sixth form as the point at which one begins to *think*—to *use* knowledge rather than merely absorb it—one must ask, again and again, *is* there a vast difference between truly intellectual activity for the young child and the old? If so, is this a difference in *degree* or in *kind*? What *are* the most effective means of improving the intellectual abilities of children and youth? To what extent is sequential learning and practice a factor in *this* area?

4. Is it reasonable to expect that significant and fundamental changes will take place in the social studies without threatening the conventional structure of education, i.e., 'the establishment'? To put it another way, *can* improvements be made by making minor changes and adjustments in the *status quo*, or is something far more radical called for?

5. Who should take the responsibility for curriculum revision in the social studies in England? Can we ask teachers to re-build curricula on their own? Should headmasters or examining boards do it? Is it possible to develop procedures that will take such work out of the realm of isolated, part-time, after-school or weekend projects? Can time and reasonable amounts of money be found to support carefully planned, long-range, regional projects as opposed to local, stop-gap measures?

6. Is it possible to interest and involve university scholars, i.e., historians, sociologists, political scientists, etc., in a meaningful way in the work of the lower schools? Can really effective curriculum revision be carried out without their help?

7. Can a child who has trouble with history spend his time just as profitably in the metal-working shop or printing room?

Is there a danger that the Newsom Report *may* be pushing English education—particularly in the social studies—towards an inferior, less challenging, and less liberalizing kind of education for the 'lower' 80 per cent of the school population? If current research indicates (and it does) that the most reasonable position for a teacher to hold today is that virtually every 'intellectual factor' *can* be developed and improved to some degree by learning, should the social studies curriculum for average and below average children be significantly different from the curriculum of *above* average children? Is it possible (if we may repeat Lawrence Cremin's challenge) 'to design . . . curricula that make no compromise with truth or significance and yet prove attractive and comprehensible to dull or poorly motivated children'?[1]

And so much for questions. Until now I have emphasized—perhaps over-emphasized—the differences between American and English education and the difficulty, therefore, of evaluating one system by the standards of the other. While such differences do exist, to be sure, a number of very real similarities exist as well. Similarly, as one views school programs dealing with the study of man and society from a world-wide, international perspective, one is struck immediately with the number of problems calling for cross-cultural, supra-national attack; problems of common interest to scholars, schoolmen and educationists in a host of nations, western and non-western, developed and developing. For example:

1. There is an almost universal need for more effective educational approaches to the problem of building closer relationships between a school's academic offerings and the eventual civic behavior of its students.

2. There is an overwhelming amount of evidence indicating that much of what is taught to children in a given country about life in *other* nations and cultures is often biased and inaccurate.

3. There is general concern about developing better ways to help children and youth learn to cope more effectively with

[1] L. Cremin, *The Genius of American Education*. Pittsburgh: University of Pittsburgh Press, 1965, p. 62.

the rapidly changing physical *and* social world in which we find ourselves.

4. Many nations are particularly concerned about the nature of *social* education programs for culturally disadvantaged children, i.e., how these children may differ from other children in terms of attitude formation, values held, learning style, etc., what their specific educational needs may be, and how to teach them more effectively.

5. There is general interest in questions concerning the political socialization of children, i.e., *what* political attitudes, knowledges and understandings are possessed by children of varying ages, *how* they are developed, and *how* the school might play a more effective role in their development.

6. There is an almost universal need for more effective means of *evaluating* both the cognitive and affective aspects of education in the humanities and social sciences.

7. There seems to be an international need for more challenging, creatively designed teaching materials of all kinds—visual, printed, manipulative, etc., to increase the effectiveness of the schools' programs in the humanities and the social sciences.

8. There is considerable interest in a number of countries in ways of improving the education of those who will ultimately teach children and youth about man and society. Teacher training institutions of all kinds are concerned about the role social science might or should play in the education of future teachers, as well as developing more effective means of helping their students to come to grips with problems of classroom application.

9. Finally, there is the problem—on an international as well as on a national scale—of closing the gap between research findings and school practices. This is related, of course, to the problem of more effective means of internationally disseminating information.

In other words, there appears to be a great deal of *overlapping* activity and effort among those working in social studies curriculum development in a number of countries including Great Britain and the United States. It seems to me that one of the most pressing needs of our time is to move beyond our own national borders as we consider the types of problems discussed in this study, sharing ideas and materials, and recognizing that, in C. E. Black's words,

> we live in a world where societies are increasingly dependent for their security on factors that extend far beyond their boundaries; where systems of production require raw materials, markets, and skills that no one country can provide; where social relationships and cultural institutions overlap national confines, and where the orientation of the individual is developing toward acquiring values that know no national frontiers.[1]

Surely the times we live in call for an *international* awakening or renaissance of interest (whichever may be appropriate) in the humanizing, liberalizing educative possibilities of the social sciences. We *know*, after all, that cruelty, bigotry, selfishness and insensitivity are *not* passed genetically from parent to child, generation through generation. We are—*all* of us—quite capable of changing our patterns of behavior. Educators everywhere, then, might take another look at the potential significance of the insights of social science for the children who will, of course, soon become the *citizens* of the world.

Perhaps Peter Odegard's summary of the possible contribution of behavioral science in general to the betterment of mankind provides both a final, fundamental argument for improved education in the social sciences and a fitting conclusion for this study as well:

> . . . men [must] choose among alternative modes of thought and behavior. It is in helping people to make these choices not as sheep but as men, not blindly in response to subliminal stimuli or visceral incitation but consciously and rationally that behavioral science can make its best contribution, knowing that human nature, no less than the physical universe about us, admits of scientific exploration and analysis, and—within limits —of guidance and control.[2]

---

[1] C. E. Black, *The Dynamics of Modernization*. New York: Harper and Row, Publishers, 1966, p. 29.

[2] Peter Odegard, 'Values and Their Communication', unpublished position paper, October, 1962, p. 7.

SUBJECT INDEX